A SCENT OF WATER

Advance Praise for *A Scent of Water...*

"The authors pose the question in the introduction, 'is Christian education worth saving?'" and go on to articulate EXACTLY why we must have solid and successful Christian education in our nation. . . . it is incumbent upon us to re-energize and reignite believers to the TRUTH that only comes through Jesus Christ. Too few children in our land are taught HIS principles or reinforced in HIS ways and it is *more important now than ever* that we not be discouraged . . . but take back lost ground. I appreciate Earwood and Suiter leading us in this great and needed work!!"
—*Chad Connelly, chairman of the South Carolina Republican Party, author, and former school board chairman*

"This book might throw cold water in your face, but keep reading! The authors have accurately summarized the history and current state of the Christian education movement and have suggested an excellent model for moving forward as schools and as a movement."
—*Dr. Jeff Walton, Executive Director, American Association of Christian Schools*

"In *A Scent of Water*, authors Suiter and Earwood strongly challenge Christian school educators to face the issues of the day in their ministry. This book will force those in positions of leadership in Christian school education to re-examine where they are at and where they need to go in order to re-gain focus in the movement called Christian school education. Today, Christians are more like the world than they realize. Biblical worldview is compromised ever so gradually. The cause is weakened, but is greater than ever as are the challenges. This work will provide inspiration to face those challenges."
—*Michael H. Bryant, EdD; Executive Director, Georgia Association of Christian Schools*

A SCENT OF WATER

Bringing Life Back to the Christian School Movement

Edward Earwood and Phil Suiter

AMBASSADOR INTERNATIONAL
GREENVILLE, SOUTH CAROLINA & BELFAST, NORTHERN IRELAND

www.ambassador-international.com

A Scent of Water
Bringing Life Back to the
Christian School Movement

Printed in the United States of America

ISBN: 978-1-62020-155-8
eISBN: 978-1-62020-154-1

Unless otherwise indicated all Scripture quotations are taken from King
James Version.

Cover design: Matthew Mulder
Typesetting: Matthew Mulder
E-book conversion: Anna Riebe

AMBASSADOR INTERNATIONAL
Emerald House
427 Wade Hampton Blvd.
Greenville, SC 29609, USA
www.ambassador-international.com

AMBASSADOR BOOKS
The Mount
2 Woodstock Link
Belfast, BT6 8DD, Northern Ireland, UK
www.ambassador-international.com

The colophon is a trademark of Ambassador

More Advance Praise for *A Scent of Water*...

"*A Scent of Water* is a must-read for any educator desiring to transform the current state of Christian education. As seasoned educators, Earwood and Suiter bring clarity to the major issues and provide an excellent blueprint for the future."

—*Joe Haas, Ed.D., Executive Director,*
North Carolina Christian School Association

"*A Scent of Water*" is exceptionally thoughtful, thorough, and Bible-based. Any school which embraces the foundational research and information and then implements the plan of action will be definitely more efficient and effective in training students to know, love, and serve the Lord Jesus in His church."

—*Dr. Cecil Beach, administrator, Northside Christian School,*
North Charleston, South Carolina

"My heart was filled with hope as I read through the pages of A Scent of Water. Certainly there is a cause, and I am excited for the Biblical principles and practical steps identified to strengthen our schools, our families, and our movement for Christ."

—*Dr. Dan Brokke, administrator, Grace Christian School,*
Huntington, West Virginia

"WOW!!! Nailed it!!! In *A Scent of Water*, Suiter and Earwood correctly identify the challenges facing the Christian school movement and offer solid ideas for bringing new life to a movement definitely worth saving. The pages are filled with scriptural application, solid research, and an action plan that offers hope for the future. "

—*Dr. Cathy Dotson, Elementary Principal,*
Wilmington Christian Academy, Wilmington, North Carolina

Contents

Acknowledgements

THE AUTHORS HAVE A NEWFOUND appreciation for the intensity of labor necessary to complete *A Scent of Water*. Like any writing project of this magnitude, numerous individuals with God-given talents have worked along with the authors to see the book through to its completion.

Kimberly Cook was most helpful in many areas of this project. From assistance with research to suggestions in areas that were not even on the radar of the authors, her encouragement and work are indelibly imprinted within.

Tim Lowry and the staff at *Ambassador International* are to be applauded for exercising gifts that transformed the content provided by the authors on a computer document into a usable format for the reader. Their assistance throughout the development of *A Scent of Water* has been invaluable. It is remarkable to see the skills that go into the writing, printing, and marketing of a book. Many thanks to those who did what the authors could never have done alone.

And to Carla McClure, the authors gratefully acknowledge that your innate gift of crafting the written word is one that has greatly enhanced our ability to communicate with the reader. It seems inadequate to simply say *thank you* when your arduous labor has made a profound difference in this book. Your knowledge of the subject matter and your keen sense of the authors' message allowed your editorial work to richly enhance our ability to communicate with the reader.

The wisest of all who have ever lived expressed the principle well in Ecclesiastes when he acknowledged that "two are better than one." He continued by noting that "a three-fold cord" was even stronger than a two-strand. The authors offer their sincere appreciation to all who have invested a thread to strengthen our cord. We shall be forever grateful.

Preface

CHRISTIAN SCHOOLING IS AT A crossroads. Student enrollment is declining, budgets for Christian schools are being cut, and the vision that originally spurred the Christian school movement seems to have faded. The question we as Christian educators must now ask ourselves is this: *Is Christian schooling worth saving?* Or, as David asked his elder brother Eliab in reminding him that God was with them in their fight against Goliath and the Philistines, "Is there not a cause?" (1 Samuel 17:29).

This question should be asked by those who waver in the discussion about the need for a strong Christian school movement. It should be asked by pastors, church leaders, and parents. It should be asked by those who train professional educators. It should be asked by everyone involved in the Christian school movement.

Is there not a cause? David was a youngster at the time he posed this question. As Israel's army contemplated the dangers and potential losses of doing battle, David apparently had insight that many around him did not possess: He had faith that the Lord would be with them in battle.

Is Christian schooling worth saving? Who among us today carries a burden for a program of education that is based upon the Word of God? Has the need for such a program lessened? Is there no longer a cause? Where is our insight? Where is our faith?

The battlefield we inhabit today is not one of swords and

slingshots, but one of worldviews. Rousas John Rushdoony warned in 1981, "A statist school can only produce a statist mind." Some fifty years ago, the Christian British philosopher Harry Blamires boldly stated, "There is no longer a Christian mind." What kind of school is needed to graduate students with a Christian mind? Is secular government likely to construct a program of public education that promotes the transformation of students' minds in the manner described by Paul (Be not conformed to this world: but be ye transformed by the renewing of your mind, that ye may prove what is that good, and acceptable, and perfect, will of God [Romans 12:2.])? We think not.

Again, we ask: *Is there a cause that is important enough to warrant the time and effort it would take to transform the Christian school movement?* Is the cause not sufficient for leaders in the movement, in colleges, in churches, and in related national, regional, and state organizations to pause and assess how the movement is faring? The starting point for addressing these questions is the Word of God, which offers a great deal of guidance to Christian educators. Consider these passages from the Bible:

> *And these words, which I command thee this day, shall be in thine heart: and thou shall teach them diligently unto thy children.*
>
> Deuteronomy 6:5-6a

> *For He established a testimony in Jacob, and appointed a law in Israel, which He commanded our fathers, that they should make them known to their children: that the generation to come might know them, even the children which should be born, who should arise and declare them to their children.*
>
> Psalm 78:5-6

Blessed [spiritually prosperous] is the man that walketh not in the counsel of the ungodly, nor standeth in the way of sinners, nor sitteth in the seat of the scornful.

Psalm 1:1

Also, consider this: Even the new birth doesn't instantly renew or reconstruct the mind of the one regenerated. When a person is reborn as a disciple of Christ, that person is cleansed of past sins, and his or her mind is opened to God's truth. However, if the mind is not properly trained through education, it will re-create many of the same errors it made before the new birth. This can be avoided if the mind can be taught the ways of God. Therefore, God has an expectation for the new believer, whether child or adult, to renew the mind, which is part of the soul of man, in the path set forth by the Word of God. Such renewal brings wisdom and discernment:

And be not conformed to this world, but be ye transformed by the renewing of your mind, that ye may prove what is that good, and acceptable, and perfect, will of God.

Romans 12:2

Solomon was blessed with profound wisdom that came directly from God. In the preamble to the book of Proverbs, he outlines what is demanded to make one wise:

To receive instruction of wisdom, justice and judgment, and equity; to give subtlety to the simple, to the young man knowledge and discretion. A wise man will hear, and will increase learning, and a man of understanding will attain unto wise counsels.

Proverbs 1:3-5

Regeneration changes the heart of the one regenerated, granting to that person a new nature, one like unto God. As stated in 2

Peter 1:4, "Whereby are given unto us exceeding great and precious promises that by these ye might be partakers of the divine nature, having escaped the corruption that is in the world through lust." This escape begins with a new birth, but it must continue with a process of education that transforms the mind, whether the mind of a child or the mind of an adult. And that education essentially means this: **developing the capacity to think as God thinks about life issues, not as the world thinks.** This kind of education is the responsibility of the family and the church, each of which has been assigned a teaching function.

So, there remains a cause, and it is this: Christian schooling requires instruction and learning that is based upon Truth. And the Lord Jesus Christ is that Truth. He is that Counsel. There is no other way to develop within children—and within learners of all ages—a mindset and heartset toward the things of God.

Christian schools are needed because education that engages the minds and hearts of learners in the things of God is not available in secular schools. Sadly, we have observed that such education is not fully available in many Christian schools either.

We realize that the previous statement may be shocking to some readers. Nevertheless, we arrived at this perspective after many years of working and serving in the Christian school movement at the national, state, and local level. Both authors have worked in a national Christian schooling organization. Each has served as an executive director of a state organization. And each has extensive experience working at the school level, leading a teaching staff, preparing for accreditation, studying achievement test results, and doing follow-up studies to determine what graduates do, once they leave Christian schools.

Our combined experiences—and our belief in the potential of Christian schooling to transform lives and improve families and communities—prompted us to ask some tough but exciting questions:

1. Why has the vision for Christian schooling faded? More important, what kind of vision and leadership is required if we hope to counter declining enrollments, school closings, and general apathy for Christian schooling?

2. What might happen if we ditch the "factory model" of education that Christian schools adopted from the secular system; incorporate new research and knowledge about education, leadership, and learning organizations; and tap the reservoir of knowledge that is possessed by professional educators working in Christian schools?

3. Why have Christian school students achieved acceptable levels of academic attainment, while graduating with a worldview that doesn't differ a great deal from the worldview of public school graduates? What might happen if we make intentional, systemic efforts to nurture both spiritual and academic development among children within the Christian school system?

This book invites you to join us in thinking about why and how to transform Christian schools so that they fill the measure of their creation. *A Scent of Water* is the fruit of many years of working with Christian schools, learning from the men and women who lead them and teach in them, and contemplating what we've seen and heard. We invite you to bring your own knowledge and experience to the book as you read. In writing the book, we spent many hours in prayer and meditation, and we invite you to consider its message prayerfully as well.

We believe there is still a cause, and there is still hope. Like David, we have faith that God is on our side. Now, we as Christian educators must collectively do what David did: act on our beliefs.

Introduction

*"For there is hope of a tree, if it be cut down, that it will sprout again, and that the tender branch thereof will not cease. Though the root thereof wax old in the earth, and the stock thereof die in the ground. **Yet through the scent of water it will bud, and bring forth boughs like a plant.**"*

Job 14:7-9

IMAGINE YOURSELF WALKING THROUGH A forest. You come upon a tree stump. Do you assume the tree is dead and finish the job by digging up the roots? Or do you water it in the hope that it will sprout new branches? Your choice will help determine the end result. The same is true for the Christian school movement, which seems to be floundering. You can either write it off as a loss and walk away, or you can nurture it and help it grow. Your choice will help determine the outcome for Christian schools and the people who work and learn within them.

Which choice will you make? The Christian mind naturally gravitates toward the second option—nourishing the root in hope of a rebirth rather than digging it up and casting it off. The potential for renewal and resurrection is, after all, central to our beliefs. But in the case of Christian schools, is it realistic to hope for a rebirth?

Absolutely! We are confident that by applying biblical principles and drawing on the best available literature on education research

17

and leadership, virtually any school can successfully transform its practice to improve the Christian schooling of children. This book elaborates on how to develop the individual and collective mindset to bring about such transformation.

The kind of transformation needed is described by Paul: "Be not conformed to this world, but be ye transformed by the renewing of your mind, that ye may prove what is that good, and acceptable, and perfect will of God" (Romans 12:2). The word *transformation* evolved from the same root as *metamorphosis*—a word that suggests a change of form, shape, structure, or substance. A true change of this sort is marked by a change of character and condition, not just outward appearance. It demands a new mindset.

Paul speaks of a substantial change of the mind so that it is not in any way conformed to the thinking of the world (e.g., as it relates to the education of children). To "conform" is to "fashion together." Paul warns us that the thinking of the believer concerning any ministry should not be fashioned together with the thinking of the world. Yet, that is exactly what we, as Christian educators, have done. We have copied the secular system, its bureaucratic administrative design, and its way of thinking about learning and about children. Why have we done this? Partly because that is all we knew at the time the Christian school movement was initiated. Perhaps we also failed to adequately search the Word of God for His views on the education of children. Unfortunately, we haven't fully "connected the dots" between Christian schooling, the high value God assigns to children, and the fact that He has a plan for each child within our care.

C. S. Lewis wrote, "There are no ordinary people. You have never talked to a mere mortal. Nations, cultures, arts, civilizations—these are mortal, and their life is to ours as the life of a gnat. But it is immortals whom we joke with, work with, marry, snub and exploit." And we hasten to add: It is immortals whom we teach in our classrooms. Each child entrusted to our care is an immortal being. Each can learn. Each deserves a quality Christian school program staffed by quality teachers capable of helping every child overcome obstacles, achieve his or her full potential, and live a life of service that gives glory to God. How can we live up to this vision?

A scent of water can be found in the Word of God—and, we humbly submit, in the research that is being done to determine what works in schools. The literature on leadership also offers powerful ideas and examples. In these resources, there is nourishment for our minds and for the Christian school movement in general. Minds and schools can be transformed.

We believe transformation is entirely possible—but not inevitable. It depends, in part, on the decisions and actions of those involved in the Christian school movement. We propose that virtually any Christian school can engage in the transformation of Christian schooling by giving appropriate attention to two matters:

First, we must recognize and support the local Christian school as the locus for all efforts to improve the academic and spiritual education of children. The local school is where "the pedal hits the metal." Regardless of how many great ideas or edicts are discussed in meetings or boardrooms, the classroom is where transformative ideas must be put into action (or not), where student needs are (or aren't) met, and where individual children benefit (or don't benefit) from receiving a Christian education. We think it is time to abandon the current bureaucratic model of leadership, which Christian schools originally adopted from secular schools. In this system, often referred to as the "factory model," decisions about education are made at upper levels of a bureaucratic system and funneled down to the level of the Christian school. Teachers within the school are viewed as something akin to assembly-line workers, responsible for imprinting management's decisions on each student as the students pass through the classroom on the K-12 conveyor belt. The factory model assumes that principals and teachers in local Christian schools can and should rush to implement directives made in board rooms far removed from the everyday realities of the classroom. *This assumption is simply false.* Furthermore, the factory model minimizes the individual gifts and needs of teachers and students alike. Opportunities for meaningful interaction, mutual support, and professional learning are being lost as teachers work in isolation from one another. That is not the nature of the body of Christ. Christian educators and leaders at the local, state, and national levels need to work together to make sure the children in our classrooms receive the education they deserve.

Second, we must develop the capacity and ability of Christian school staff members to function as an effective professional learning community. A professional learning community is an organizational design that taps into the strengths, the skills, and the abilities of a school's staff to design instructional and curricular systems that will meet the spiritual and academic needs of students. A professional learning community promotes a shared mission, a shared vision, and shared values among the staff. Collective inquiry becomes a tool for discerning systemic problems. Teams of teachers work collaboratively to solve problems and come up with solutions. Collaborating teams of educators test possible solutions to the problems they see. Decisions are made on the basis of data that show how well students are learning. The school principal becomes more than a manager; he or she becomes a capacity builder who provides faculty members with the training, resources, and opportunities they need to develop their professional abilities and to function within a learning community. Professional learning communities commit to continuous improvement. They can initiate changes in the culture of a school, and they take a deep systemic approach toward improving the education of children.

We believe that recognizing the important role of each Christian school and building the capacity of each school faculty to collaborate effectively are essential to moving the ministry of Christian schooling forward. No doubt, it will be challenging work. But it can also be tremendously rewarding. And it can be done. The chapters that follow will help you consider possibilities and take appropriate actions as you become part of the transformation.

Chapter 1 describes the Christian school movement as it exists today. We do not offer these statements as indictments. They are merely descriptions of conditions that currently characterize the movement. Although some of these realities seem great, keep in mind that none are impossible to overcome.

Chapter 2 provides an overview of the federal government's efforts to transform public education in the United States, from the Excellence Movement to the Restructuring Movement and its emphasis on national goals to the Accountability Movement that established achievement standards for public schools. We examine the administrative model employed in these reform programs and make applications to the Christian school movement.

Chapter 3 introduces the concept of professional learning communities as vehicles for systemic change and explains why and how creating professional learning communities within local Christian schools is one of the keys to transforming Christian schooling. We also introduce the reader to the component technologies of a changed Christian school.

Chapter 4 discusses Bible-based leadership principles and their application in a Christian school setting. Servant-leadership, coupled with a strong testimony of righteousness, is the foundation for effective administration. Chapter 5 presents a new vision for the responsibilities of school leaders engaged in transforming the Christian school movement. In this view, the principal assumes responsibility for cultivating the leadership potential of each person working within the ministry. The principal supports staff members as they build their own knowledge, skills, and dispositions; ensures program coherence and identifies the technical resources that are needed; and builds his or her own leadership skills and ability to function in a professional learning community.

Chapters 6 and 7 discuss the foundation that must be put in place for every Christian school. This foundation is embodied in written documents that define a philosophy of Christian schooling, a moral purpose or mission statement for the school, a vision for the school at some time in the future, general goals, and a values statement describing how the professional staff of the school will behave as the program of education is carried out.

Chapter 8 describes a new pedagogy for a transformed Christian school movement. It offers a dynamic description of what a teacher does while serving in a professional learning community, highlighting the need for flexibility to teach adaptively while building positive relationships with other faculty members and the students. The chapter addresses the need for teachers to be life-long learners, to work as members of teams, and to help develop a guaranteed and viable curriculum.

Chapter 9 discusses the critical nature of professional development for the staff of a Christian school. Such development is vital to the effectiveness of the Christian school ministry. In transformed schools, professional development is not a "sit and get" or "go and get" experience; rather, it's embedded in the everyday routines and realities of teaching and learning. It requires the active participation of all professional staff members within a collegial environment.

Chapter 10 explores ways parents can become effectively involved in the Christian school and more active in the education of their own children. The Bible assigns parents the major responsibility for rearing and educating children. Christian school personnel cannot replace parents, but they can assist parents in fulfilling this responsibility in a variety of ways.

Chapter 11 addresses the question *Where do we go from here?* There we describe nine shifts in thinking that are critical to transforming Christian schooling. We also propose specific roles and actions for national, regional, and state organizations and for the colleges that prepare teachers and education administrators.

Given the growing complexity of life in the twenty-first century, we believe Christian schooling is more important than ever. Bringing "a scent of water" to the movement is more important than casting blame or concerning ourselves with turf battles. Transforming Christian schools is serious work that will demand— and develop—spiritual maturity. Those engaged in this work will need to seek God's will and vision concerning the role of Christian schools in today's world. As Solomon said, "Where there is no vision, the people perish: but he that keepeth the law, happy is he" (Proverbs 29:18). For the believer, *happiness* means spiritual prosperity. That is what Christian schooling is designed to help young people accomplish.

CHAPTER I

Ten Realities about Christian Schooling

Ye are not straitened in us, but ye are straitened in your own bowels.

2 Corinthians 6:12

We have met the enemy, and he is us.

Walt Kelley (1970)

THE MINISTRY OF CHRISTIAN SCHOOLING is endangered. As student enrollment continues to decline, budgets are being cut, and downsizing is a frequent topic of discussion in our board rooms. For those of us who think Christian schooling can and should play an important role in preparing young people to serve God and humankind, this trend is troubling. Yet, it need not cause despair. If the Lord wants us to reverse the trend so that Christian schooling can once again flourish, and if we are willing to do the spiritual and temporal work necessary to transform Christian schools, then a turnaround is entirely possible.

To initiate a turnaround or revival of Christian schooling, we must honestly ask ourselves two questions: (1) Who or what is hindering the Christian school movement from thriving and moving forward? and (2) What realities must the movement address if it's to be revitalized?

In his second epistle to the church at Corinth, the Apostle Paul addressed a question similar to the first one. Many Corinthian church members felt they weren't thriving as they should, and some blamed Paul and other church leaders. Paul told them, "Ye are not straitened in us, but ye are straitened in your own bowels" (2 Corinthians 6:12). In other words, he said their spiritual growth was not being restricted or squeezed ("straitened") by him or other church leaders, but by their own passions and desires ("bowels")— by their own wants and their own limitations in knowledge and understanding. Some 2,000 years later, cartoonist Walt Kelley, creator of the Pogo comic strip, summed it up like this: "We have met the enemy, and he is us."

Who or what is hindering the Christian school movement from thriving and moving forward? It's not competition from sectarian schools or a lessening need for Christian schooling. *It's our own actions (or inactions) within the movement.* The movement is weakened every time school leaders hire teachers who are not prepared to carry out the ministry, or when leaders don't support teachers' meaningful professional growth. It's weakened when colleges and universities graduate teacher candidates who don't know how to manage classrooms or provide effective instruction. It's weakened when school leaders and faculty members think "I know enough about teaching and learning and have no need to know more." It's weakened when parents make half-hearted attempts to educate their children according to principles found in the Word of God. It's weakened when students who don't understand their own divine natures enter Christian schools that don't have a vision of their own divine missions. In short, the Christian school movement is weakened when we lose our passion for the ministry, and thus lose the great blessing of the Lord: *We have met the enemy, and he is us.*

What realities must the movement address if Christian schooling is to be revitalized? In his address to the Corinthians, Paul gently urged church members to face the facts and assume responsibility for their own spiritual growth. In his bestselling book *Good to Great*, Jim Collins (2001) recommends a similar approach. *Good to Great* is about eleven companies that significantly improved their performance over time. Collins and a team of researchers discovered that these companies had at least one thing in common: "a corporate culture that rigorously found and promoted disciplined people to think and act in a disciplined manner." Part of that discipline involved leaders who insisted on facing what Collins calls "the brutal facts" about their company's performance. These leaders didn't hesitate to ask who or what was keeping the company from achieving its goals. Instead, "they hit the realities of their situation head-on."

Collins rightly cautions that the transformation of an organization does not begin when leaders jump on the bandwagon of trends or fads set by others. It begins when leaders and other interested parties jointly examine the data in front of them. Everyone who holds a stake or interest in Christian schooling should involve themselves in this process, including leaders of national, state, and regional organizations; school administrators and teachers; faculty in colleges of teacher education; and parents. All of us need to look at the reality of Christian schooling today and compare that reality to the vision we have for what Christian schooling could or should be. The creative tension between "what is" and "what could be" can move us to breathe new life into the system.

So what are the realities or "brutal facts" that we must face if we hope to revive Christian schooling? Based on the authors' years of experience in Christian schooling at the national, state, and local levels, combined with readings in education research and leadership, we have identified realities about Christian schooling that we believe must be addressed. You may not agree with our list, and you may think of additional issues not included here. We invite you to use the list as a starting point for your own thinking. As you read the discussion that follows, consider how each of these realities might affect the quality of education delivered in Christian schools today.

REALITY #1: **The Christian school movement began as a knee-jerk reaction to social changes.**

Prior to the major social changes of the mid-twentieth century, much of the culture of the United States, including its system of public education, was informed by Christian values. But as World War II came to an end, things were changing. The age of modernity had come—an age characterized by "the guiding hope that, given enough time and energy, human beings could experience the world, think hard, and come up with reliable answers, correct answers, regarding the nature of things. Here was a powerful confidence that all persons of goodwill, sufficient gifts (whether in intelligence, aesthetic sensibility, and so on), and appropriate skill can examine the pertinent data and come to the same true conclusions" (Stackhouse, 2002).

This new spirit of modernity pervaded the entire culture and began to reshape the way people thought about the education of children. Oliver Wendell Holmes once said, "You create a just society based on universal human reason." Modernity's worship of reason and rejection of faith removes the Word of God as a defining factor in shaping social institutions, including the education system. The mind of man—not the Word of God—would become our society's moral compass. Modernity discounts the value of a worldview based upon Scripture and greatly elevates the importance of critical thinking and human reasoning.

As this new worldview rippled its way across society's institutions, the resulting social changes of the 1960s and 1970s were met by pastors and Christian parents with much alarm. There was a rush to seek the approval of legislation defining the conditions under which private Christian schools could operate. There was a rush to open Christian schools all across the nation. The rush was a knee-jerk reaction to what was happening in the broader culture. Those leading the charge didn't have time to reflect on how to organize and staff schools according to biblical principles. So they adopted the public education model and many of the philosophies that governed it. Christian schools opened at a rapid pace. Little time was devoted to planning, and principals and teachers were often unprepared for their roles.

Unfortunately, although decades have passed, many Christian schools and staffs remain unprepared to teach—and are unguided by a sound scriptural mandate. One often hears this reasoning: *No matter what we do, we are better than the alternative.* This line of thinking makes public schools the yardstick by which the success of Christian schools is measured. Don't you think the Lord expects more than that? The only standard for Christian schooling should be excellence, and the level of excellence to which we aspire must be defined by biblical truth.

REALITY #2: **The movement lacks a clear philosophy and theology of education for children.**

Much of what has been done in the Christian school movement has not been guided by a clear philosophy of Christian schooling that is based on a thorough study of the Word of God. What does the Bible have to say about children; their relationship to parents, to teachers, and to God; and their make-up in terms of body, soul, and spirit? What does the Bible have to say about knowledge and the place of knowledge in making one wise?

Every legislature in the United States deals with the issue of who "owns" the child as lawmakers address issues of education. What rights do the several states have in the lives of children living within the state? Does God have a compelling interest in the lives of the children? Does the state? If so, what is that compelling interest? In many places, the state and the teachers union openly declare that the state owns the child for purposes of education. Then, what is the role of the local church in the education of children, and how does that role relate to the responsibility that the Bible gives to parents over their children? If God owns the child (and He does: see Ezekiel 18:4, Psalm 24:1, and Romans 14:7-8), what does God expect of parents? If mankind has been given stewardship over the earth, to *"be fruitful, and multiply, and replenish the earth and subdue it: and have dominion over...every living thing that moveth upon the earth"* (Genesis 1:29), how should the youth of our nation be prepared to exercise this responsibility?

It is incumbent upon leaders in the Christian school movement to develop a clear understanding of the biblical principles of leadership and stewardship. These principles should be clearly articulated as they relate to educating young people. They should be contemplated, discussed, and consulted by those making decisions about teaching, learning, and administration. If written in short form, in plain language, they could serve as discussion starters among pastors, educators, parents, and others interested in the movement. Currently, however, no such document exists, and many Christian educators find it difficult to put into words the uniquely Christian philosophy and theology on which they base (or should base) their decisions and actions in the school and in the classroom.

REALITY #3: **Leaders within the movement have generally failed to establish a mission and vision for Christian schooling.**

Educators Robert DuFour and Richard Eaker (1998) say that writing a mission/purpose statement and a vision statement are essential to establishing a learning community—a group of people united in purpose who are committed to learning together in order to better achieve their joint goals. In his book *Good to Great*, researcher Jim Collins (2001) discusses a related idea he calls The Hedgehog Concept—a deliberate, laser-like focus on what your organization can do better than any other. Such focus makes it easier to accomplish a complex process (such as educating children) because it unifies and guides everything that is done within a school or other organization. Few Christian schools have developed mission and vision statements that embody The Hedgehog Concept. Few national and state organizations have sensed the need to help administrators and staffs of local schools to do it. J. Bardwick (1996) states the idea very succinctly: "The most important question in any organization has to be 'what is the business of our business?' Answering this question is the first step in setting priorities."

The authors have visited numerous Christian schools, from Hawaii to New England. In our experience, it is rare to find a clear statement of mission and purpose. It is even more rare to find a vision statement that expresses passion for the work the school is doing, or that clearly states where the principal, teachers, and parents desire the school to be at some time in the future. There is a great need for understanding what mission and vision statements are, why it's important to involve all stakeholders in developing and periodically refining such statements, and how to translate them into everyday actions.

REALITY #4: **The level of pastoral leadership in the movement has diminished.**

In the mid- to late 1970s, one of the coauthors of this book held a very responsible position in a state education agency, where he directed the division that oversaw the day-to-day operation of the public schools within the state system. At that time, it was not uncommon for pastors to visit the office, inquiring about how to start Christian schools. Many wanted to know about the authority of the state, if any, over the operation of the future school. These pastors were concerned about helping the parents and children within their congregations. They quickly became leaders in the Christian school movement.

Today, however, pastors seem to have lost their passion for educating children in a Christian setting. The question of the church's role in educating children may be debatable. One can certainly build a strong biblical case for that function first belonging to parents. But it was pastors who assumed a share of that burden as the Christian school movement began in the late 1960s and 1970s. Now, there seems to be an absence of pastoral leadership for education, even in church-affiliated schools. Why the shift? Perhaps the pastors of sponsoring churches are suffering from burnout. Or maybe they're disappointed with the outcomes. Some pastors openly state that they no longer want anything to do with a Christian school. Regardless of the reason, the reality is this: Pastors have removed themselves from this movement in growing numbers at a time when strong visionary leadership is needed. Joan Fitzpatrick (2002), in an unpublished dissertation at Regents University, concluded that Christian schools close because of a loss of quality leadership and the homogeneity of vision and culture. Burnout is a factor, and it has an impact on the quality of leadership. This finding is worth studying, especially since it comes at a time when many pastors may be suffering from burnout and voluntarily removing themselves from active involvement in the Christian school movement.

REALITY #5: **National and state leaders have inadequately defined their respective roles.**

There are at least four major national organizations seeking to provide leadership in the Christian school movement. These organizations maintain some kind of affiliation with state or regional organizations. Schools hold some kind of membership or relationship with the national or regional group. Yet there has been little if any attempt to define the respective and logical roles for these organizations. Two important questions should be asked: *What is a national association able to do that a state or regional affiliate organization is not able to do? What is a state organization able to do better and more cost effectively than a national or regional organization?* These questions are logical, and they can be answered. Yet, largely because of political issues or turf battles, they do not get asked. Because important questions remain unaddressed, there is often a strained relationship among local, state, regional, and national organizations.

What's needed is systemic thinking—a type of big-picture thinking that reflects an in-depth understanding of how the various components of a system influence one another to create a result. Each school is a system that encompasses administrators, teachers, and students (and, by extension, their parents). In turn, the Christian school movement is a system that encompasses national, state, regional, and local leaders. To be effective, systemic thinking must lead to appropriate collaborative actions, and these actions must be guided by a clear vision and mission for Christian schooling.

REALITY #6: **Administrative leadership at the school level lacks the training necessary to lead improvements in teaching and learning.**

In the thirty years that the authors of this book have been involved in the Christian school movement, we've had many opportunities to observe how decisions are made regarding school leadership. All too often, the decision about who would serve as the principal of a newly opened Christian school was made on the basis of who had the most time available or who ranked lowest on the so-called totem pole. The truth is this: Current options are limited because the cadre of ready-and-able individuals who have been trained to perform the role of Christian school principal is very small. Further, very few individuals are seeking the preparation needed to serve as an effective Christian school principal. The situation is so dire that institutions that offer such preparation are cutting back or even closing their programs.

Leading a Christian school is a distinct profession that requires specialized knowledge and skills. One distinction of a *profession* is the existence of a body of knowledge that one needs to serve in a particular professional role. Another is the presence of leaders who have produced literature to describe the professional role—literature that helps define preparation programs as well as service within the profession. It appears that, on both counts, the Christian school movement has major voids.

The Christian school movement can be revitalized and sustained only if we prepare school leaders as professionals who understand the very core of educational practice—the nature of knowledge, the student's role in learning, and how these ideas about knowledge and learning are manifested in the behavior of the teacher, especially in teaching method and class work. There must be school principals with the training to join and lead a teaching faculty in the collaborative work of learning with and from one another how to better serve students. Presently, very few Christian school principals have the training they need to perform in this role.

REALITY #7: **The movement lacks a strong commitment to excellence in education.**

Results of the Stanford Achievement Test (SAT), which is administered annually in public schools and in many Christian schools, show that students in Christian schools perform higher than the national norm in all subject areas. This is as it should be, given that the parents of students who attend Christian schools elect to pay a significant tuition bill—and these parents generally have high aspirations for their children and high expectations of the school staff.

However, Christian educators should be careful about how much they gloat about SAT results. For one thing, the SAT is only one way of measuring what students know. For another, the SAT is a norm-referenced test. This type of test measures student performance against that of other students—not against a standard of performance that remains constant over time. The SAT norms are updated about once a decade, which means the norm is based on achievement levels at the time the norm was updated. In some cases, actual achievement at the 90th percentile in 2010 is considerably less that the 90th percentile in 1970.

Should the standard for Christian schools be whether we're "better than today's (or yesterday's) public schools"? In our work with Christian schools, we (the authors) have often heard the sentiment expressed that *no matter what we do, it is better than the public system.* But shouldn't we be aiming for something higher? If there is a standard by which we should judge ourselves, shouldn't it be a standard set by God Himself? And wouldn't that standard be *excellence*?

REALITY #8: **There has been a failure to adequately prepare enough educators to sustain the Christian school movement.**

Volumes of research attest to the significant role of vision, mission, and values; to the impact of a competent teaching staff in schools; to the critical need for leadership within the context of a learning community; and to the importance of synergy in developing and maintaining school improvements. If the ministry of Christian schooling is to be revitalized, addressing teacher preparation in a synergistic way is essential.

Synergy is *the interaction between two or more agents or forces so that the combined effect is greater than the sum of their individual effects.* Synergy with regard to teacher preparation is sorely needed within the Christian school movement. Part of the problem is lack of meaningful, ongoing communication and coordination among national, state, and local education leaders; faculty at teacher preparation colleges; and practitioners at the local school level. This type of synergy revolves around a clearly articulated vision and mission statement, and it must be supported by leaders focused on building the capacity of everyone involved for the purpose of accomplishing the mission. Teacher preparation is an essential component of such capacity building.

REALITY #9: **Too many students who graduate from Christian schools do not embrace a biblical worldview.**

One would think that the acquisition of a worldview or lifeview based on the truth of Scripture would be among the major purposes for the Christian school movement. But data on graduates of traditional Christian schools in the United States indicate that this goal is not being achieved. In fact, in terms of having a biblical worldview, graduates of traditional Christian schools have trended downward over the past twenty-two years or since that goal has been tested.

This observation is based, in part, on the results of the PEERS test, which is produced by the Nehemiah Institute (nehemiahinstitute.com). More than 100,000 students have taken this test, which is designed to assess a person's worldview on politics, economics, education, religion, and social issues. Analysis of PEERS test results show that:

- The worldview score of a typical graduate of a traditional Christian school falls just slightly above that of public school graduates.
- A sizeable percentage of Christian school teachers possess a secular worldview.
- The understanding of principles of education as found in the Bible is lower among Christian educators than among the general Christian population.

Though some will not accept these data because of the particular theological slant of the test, they are the best data available on the worldview of both students and professionals involved in Christian schooling. The results are disturbing. It appears that many traditional Christian schools are failing at the task of instilling in students a worldview that is based on the Word of God.

REALITY #10: **The movement is hampered by insufficient financial support.**

Although the focus of this work does not include direct attention to the financial challenges encountered by many ministries, we do believe that to ignore this "elephant in the room" is to ignore the obvious reality that faces most school leaders. In fact, the issue of appropriate and adequate funding is so expansive that it deserves its own study; thorough examination and research must be given to the financial well-being of educational ministries if the Christian school movement is to maintain significance and influence in coming days. We encourage a thorough examination of the financial health of the movement; it is our belief that significant change that only results from "outside the box" thinking is needed. For this reason, we have focused our work on the programmatic aspects of Christian school operation—new views of school leadership and curriculum, the importance of a school's foundation and culture, and re-defining the role of faculty. *Learning* should be the focus of everything that is done in the Christian school, but we recognize that, just like learning will fail without a solid foundation, so too will the Christian school without a solid financial foundation.

Where Do We Go From Here?

The ten realities of Christian schooling presented in this chapter represent the authors' view of "where we are" as opposed to "where we need to be". This view is based on our many years of experience at all levels of the Christian schooling system. Leading the Christian school movement from here (*what is*) to there (*what could be*) will require not only vision but also the courage to confront the "brutal facts" of the situation—and to act upon the implications of those facts. To take appropriate action, Collins (2001) advocates creating a climate where the truth is heard and where these four basic practices dominate:

1. Lead with questions, not answers.
2. Engage in dialogue and debate, not coercion.
3. Conduct autopsies without assigning blame.
4. Build red flag mechanisms that turn *information* into *information that cannot be ignored.*

These practices call on leaders to practice biblical principles: It takes humility and courage for servant-leaders to ask questions and to consider answers other than their own. It takes patience and brotherly love to do things *with* others instead of *to* them. It takes discipline and pure intent to honestly assess a situation without casting blame. It takes wisdom and an understanding of God's will to set priorities and to communicate those priorities so that they can't be misunderstood or ignored.

We believe that developing and practicing these leadership principles can help all of us work together to revive the Christian school movement. We've described the movement as a noble journey embarked on years ago without much planning and without a good road map. Now that we've reached a crossroads, it's time to consider how we got here, refuel, make sure we have a map based on the Word of God, and faithfully resume the journey.

CHAPTER 2

School Reform: Boom or Bust?

A wise man will hear, and will increase learning; a man of understanding shall attain unto wise counsels.

King Solomon, Proverbs 1:2-5

A TREMENDOUS AMOUNT OF RESEARCH has been done within the public system of education in the United States in an effort to discover ways to improve the quality of the system and its outcomes. By contrast, very few studies have examined the outcomes or the processes of education that occur daily in private Christian schools. Might the Christian school movement benefit from a careful review of the research being done in the public system on teaching, learning, and educational leadership? It's a question worth asking.

Perhaps the best-known report on public education research is the one released by the National Commission of Excellence in Education in 1983. This commission, appointed by President Ronald Reagan, examined educational content, expectations, use of time, and teaching. The findings were reported in *A Nation at Risk* (National Commission on Excellence in Education, 1983). The report startled national leaders, including the president, by describing the American education system as being in a state of crisis. The most often quoted passage from that report states, "*If an unfriendly foreign power had attempted to impose on America the mediocre educational performance that exists today, we might well have viewed it as an act of war.*"

A Nation at Risk sparked three major education reform movements by the federal government. What follows is an overview of those initiatives and related research findings about their results. Next, we present data on the results of Christian schools. As you read, ask yourself, *What lessons can be learned from recent efforts to improve public schools? If we want to reform or renew Christian schools, where should we focus our attention? What processes are most likely to bring about meaningful changes in teaching and learning?*

The Excellence Movement

The initial response to *A Nation at Risk* was a school reform initiative often referred to as The Excellence Movement. The Excellence Movement did not address systemic change in the schools. There was no emphasis on examining the culture of the school. There was no examination of the nature of the leadership provided by principals and superintendents. There was no opportunity for the teaching staff to jointly consider needed improvements in the school. There was no broadening of the decision-making base as school improvements were considered.

Rather, state boards of education and the education committees of state legislatures emphasized the addition of common requirements: More credits were required for graduation. Courses were made more rigorous. More days were added to school calendars. Teacher preparation programs in colleges were modified to require more semester or quarter hours for state certification. Even grading scales were modified. Stated simply, standards and other requirements already characterizing the schools were intensified—but the emphasis was on doing *more of the same* rather than something different.

Some five years after The Excellence Movement was initiated,

President Reagan hosted a ceremony in the East Room of the White House to highlight and celebrate the school reform initiatives that had been undertaken. Edward Fiske, former education editor for the *New York Times,* was among those in attendance. Fiske (1992) wrote the following words shortly thereafter:

> *Leading politicians and educators, as well as those in the national media who cover education, used the occasion to reflect on the accomplishments of school reform. And we came to a startling conclusion:* **There weren't any.**

Actually, data published by the National Center for Education Statistics (1995) indicate some improvement on selected measures. For example, in 1994, high school students were taking more courses, including a greater number of more difficult courses. Furthermore, there was some improvement in mathematics and science achievement. And it didn't seem that the reform did any harm. The increases in academic course taking did not adversely affect the achievement of advanced students; nor did students with lower abilities suffer as a result of curricular reforms. Overall, however, no significant and lasting increase in achievement can be attributed to the Excellence Movement.

What happened? Why did the Excellence Movement fail to yield the hoped-for results? At least part of the explanation lies in the movement's "top-down" approach that had little chance of changing the basic nature of the education system. Few new ideas were offered, and there was little effort to reach the school level with the incentives and support necessary to improve the quality of education offered in America's classrooms ("where the pedal hits the metal"). In retrospect, The Excellence Movement amounted to a knee-jerk response to the findings of the National Commission on Excellence in Education. Its perpetuation of the factory model of schooling, with its emphasis on "changing the rules" rather than "changing the culture," had almost no hope of significantly altering the way education is done in the United States. Alsalam and Ogle (1990) concluded that *"stagnation at relatively low levels appears to describe the level of performance of American students."*

The Restructuring Movement

The disappointing results of The Excellence Movement prompted a new national school reform initiative. The Restructuring Movement began on March 31, 1994, when President Bill Clinton signed into law the Goals 2000: Educate America Act (P. L. 103-227). The act was based on the premise that students will reach higher levels of achievement when more is expected of them. Congress appropriated $105 million for Goals 2000 for the fiscal year 1994.

Goals 2000 codified into law six education goals related to school readiness, school completion, student academic achievement, leadership in math and science, adult literacy, and safe and drug-free schools. Two additional goals were later added to encourage teacher professional development and parental participation. Here's a summary of the goals, which were to be accomplished by the year 2000 (Paris, 1994):

1. All children in America will start school ready to learn.
2. The high school graduation rate will increase to at least 90 percent.
3. All students will leave grades 4, 8, and 12 having demonstrated competency over challenging subject matter, including English, mathematics, science, foreign languages, civics, economics, the arts, history, and geography, and every school in America will ensure that all students learn to use their minds well, so they may be prepared for responsible citizenship, further learning, and productive employment in our nation's modern economy.
4. U.S. students will be first in the world in mathematics

and science achievement.

5. Every adult American will be literate and will possess the knowledge and skills necessary to compete in a global economy and exercise the rights and responsibilities of citizenship.

6. Every school in America will be free of drugs, violence, and the unauthorized presence of firearms and alcohol and will offer a disciplined environment conducive to learning.

7. The nation's teaching force will have access to programs for the continued improvement of their professional skills and the opportunity to acquire the knowledge and skills needed to instruct and prepare all American students for the next century.

8. Every school will promote partnerships that will increase parental involvement and participation in promoting the social, emotional, and academic growth of children.

With Goals 2000, the push to establish voluntary national standards began in earnest. The act established a National Education Standards and Improvement Council to examine and certify national and state content, student performance, and assessment systems voluntarily submitted by several states. The effort to develop voluntary standards for several subject areas was financed by the federal government.

To its credit, Goals 2000 focused on site-based reform, giving attention to such things as building-level leadership vested with the authority over staffing, the curriculum, and even aspects of budgeting; shared responsibility for decisions; shared planning time by those having direct responsibility for student instruction; and heterogeneous grouping in core subjects (Newmann & Associates, 1996). Goals 2000 presented building administrators and their teaching staffs with an opportunity to use their knowledge of pedagogy more creatively to better serve their students and schools. Moreover, the federal government provided huge amounts of money that could be used to promote the modifications necessary to improve the education product. Throughout the education system, there was "confidence that teachers and principals, with the help of parents and students, can get their own school house in order" (Barth, 1990).

But even a casual observer can tell you that the eight goals of the Educate America Act were not achieved. A report published by the Heritage Foundation (Lips, 2008) reviewed Goals 2000 and other education reform efforts, and concluded:

> *The American education system remains in a state of crisis. Each year, the United States spends more than $550 billion on K-12 public schools—more than four percent of the nation's gross domestic product…. Regrettably, millions of American students continue to pass through the nation's public schools without receiving a quality education. On the 2007 National Assessment of Education Progress (NAEP) test, thirty-three percent of fourth-grade students scored "below basic" in reading. Among economically disadvantaged children, fifty percent scored "below basic" in reading. In many of the nation's largest cities, high school graduation rates are below fifty percent.*

Why did this massive, well-funded effort fall short of its mark? For one thing, the Restructuring Movement assumed that establishing a new decision-making structure would translate into new and better practices in the classroom. But, as Joseph Murphy and others (1991) had observed even before the movement began,

> *The connections between teacher empowerment and site-based management and improved education processes and outcomes are tenuous at best…. It remains to be seen if restructuring*

leads to radical changes that deeply affect teachers and students or if changes will stop at the classroom door, leaving the teaching-learning process largely unaltered.

Reform efforts under the Restructuring Movement gave too much attention to changes in school organization that do not directly address the quality of student learning. As Newmann and Wehlage (1995) point out, new administrative arrangements and teaching techniques contribute to improved learning only if they are carried out within a framework that focuses on learning of high intellectual quality. Reform under the Restructuring Movement seldom challenged school staff members to change their teaching practices.

Dufour and Eaker (1998) found that school improvement agendas during the Restructuring Movement tended to drift to nonacademic administration issues. Three issues repeatedly surfaced:

1. **Student discipline:** How can we get the students to behave better in our school?
2. **Parental involvement:** How can we get parents to accept greater responsibility for their child's learning?
3. **Faculty morale:** How can we ensure that the adults who work in our school feel good about their working conditions?

Notice that what matters most—teaching and learning—didn't make it to the top of the list.

Thus, the Restructuring Movement failed to improve the schools of this nation in a major way. The eight goals of Goals 2000 were not achieved by 2000, and they remain unachieved today. Even when local school staffs were provided opportunities to work on matters of school culture, improvement did not necessarily occur. Why? *Because the know-how was simply not there.*

The Accountability Movement

The next major thrust of the federal government was the Accountability Movement, launched on January 8, 2002, when President George W. Bush signed into law the No Child Left Behind Act (NCLB). NCLB was the eighth reauthorization of the Elementary and Secondary Education Act (ESEA), originally passed in 1965 as a part of President Lyndon B. Johnson's War on Poverty. This federal legislation has been central to K-12 school reform efforts since that date. NCLB was based on the belief that setting high standards, establishing measurable goals, and holding schools accountable for students' progress (or lack of progress) can result in improved individual outcomes for students.

NCLB's testing requirement applies to all government-run schools and to all states that receive federal funding. A statewide standardized test is administered annually, with all students taking the same test under the same conditions (with a limited number of exceptions and exclusions). Test results are used to determine whether a school is eligible for Title I funding through ESEA. These results serve as a measure of adequate yearly progress (AYP). For example, there is the expectation that students at any grade level must achieve higher than the previous year's students at that grade level.

Under NCLB, schools that fail to achieve adequate yearly progress for two consecutive years are labeled "in need of improvement" and are required to develop a two-year improvement plan for the subject area(s) in which student achievement does not meet the AYP requirement. Students in such schools are given the option of transferring to another school within the school district. Failure to meet the AYP expectation for a third year forces the school to offer free tutoring and other supplemental education opportunities for those children. If a school doesn't achieve AYP for a fourth year, the school is labeled as requiring "corrective action," which might involve such actions as a wholesale replacement of the teaching staff, introduction of a new curriculum, or extending time the students actually spend on task.

A fifth year of failure to achieve AYP requires a plan to restructure the entire school, with the plan being implemented if the school fails to reach the desired AYP for a sixth consecutive year. Common options include closing the school, turning it into a charter school, or hiring a private contractor to operate the school. In the case of some states, it would mean the state education agency taking over and operating the school.

NCLB has drawn much criticism because of its heavy reliance on tests and the narrowness of that measure of student achievement. It should be said that NCLB has directed greater attention to low-achieving schools and sparked intensified efforts to improve persistently low-performing schools.

When researchers Jennings and Rentner (2006) examined the impact of test-driven accountability under the provisions of (NCLB), they identified ten effects:

1. State and district officials report that student achievement on state tests is rising, though it is not clear that students are gaining as much as rising percentages of proficiency scores would suggest.
2. Schools are spending more time on reading and math, sometimes at the expense of subjects not tested.
3. Schools are paying much more attention to the alignment of curriculum and instruction and are analyzing test score data more closely.
4. Low-performing schools are undergoing makeovers rather than the most radical kinds of restructuring outlined in No Child Left Behind.
5. Schools and teachers have made considerable progress in demonstrating that teachers meet the law's academic qualifications.
6. Students are taking many more tests.

7. Schools are paying much more attention to achievement gaps and the learning needs of particular groups of students.

8. The percentage of schools on state "needs improvement" lists has been steady but not increasing.

9. The federal government is playing a larger role in education.

10. Because of NCLB requirements, state governments and school districts also have expanded roles in school operations, but often without adequate federal funds to carry out their duties.

On March 9, 2011, *Education Week* reported on an interview with U.S. Secretary of Education Arne Duncan, who said that "unless changes are made to a key facet of the Elementary and Secondary Education Act (NCLB), the country is on track to see 82 percent of its schools labeled 'failing' this year" (McNeil, 2011, p. 1). The Secretary was referring specifically to the requirement for schools to meet the pre-established "adequate yearly progress" or AYP targets. Failure to meet those targets will mean that states and districts will have to intervene directly in schools.

On March 15, 2011, Jennifer Marshall, Director of Domestic Policy Studies for the Heritage Foundation, testifying before the House of Representatives Education Committee, said:

> *A half century of always expanding and ever shifting federal intervention into local schools has failed to improve achievement. But it has caused an enormous compliance burden. The damage isn't just wasted dollars and human capital that could have more effectively achieved educational excellence. It has also undermined direct accountability to parents and taxpayers while encouraging bureaucratic expansion and empowering special interests.*

Once again, we ask: *Why?* Why has NCLB resulted in no major improvement in student achievement levels? Why is the graduation rate still a problem? At least part of the answer lies in its unstated assumptions about what schools are: Setting high standards, writing measurable goals, tracking progress, and holding organizations accountable for results might seem like a reasonable formula for improving productivity—if schools were factories. But schools aren't factories. Students aren't merely "raw material" moving along a conveyor belt. And teachers aren't assembly line workers hired to follow lofty mandates as they filter downward through the educational bureaucracy through local boards of education, superintendents, and principals. Schools are communities with their own histories and cultures, and they are inhabited by diverse human beings who bring to the table their individual strengths, goals, dreams, and abilities. NCLB doesn't take this into account. Neither does the law help members of the school community examine and (as appropriate) modify their individual and collective mental constructs regarding the purpose and process of educating children. In short, there is no provision for building capacity and developing synergy at the school level.

The Legacy of Public School Reform Movements

In 2008, U.S. Secretary of Education Margaret Spellings reviewed progress made during the twenty-five years since the publication of *A Nation at Risk*. She reached four sobering conclusions:

- If we were "at risk" in 1983, we are at even greater risk now. The education system is not keeping pace with growing demands.
- Of twenty children born in 1983, six did not graduate from high school on time in 2001. Of the fourteen who did, ten started college that fall, but only five earned a bachelor's degree by spring 2007.

- The nation has finally been awakened to the condition of its school system.
- There is a need to leverage this information to achieve better results.

Perhaps the most important legacy of *A Nation at Risk* was this: It resonated with the citizens of the United States. It put the quality of public education on the national political agenda, and it has remained there ever since (Fiske, 1992). The report also caused a stir among many Bible-believing Christians, who began to ask serious questions about the education of their children, whether they attended public schools or private Christian schools.

The Christian School/Home School Movement

Some fifty to sixty years ago, nearly all U.S. schools reflected a religious bent in their philosophies and in their operation. But, the cultural upheavals of the 1960s and 1970s changed all of that. To counter these social and cultural changes and the humanistic philosophies pervading the public schools, there began a movement to open private Christian schools all across the nation. Legislation was approved by many state legislatures defining the conditions under which private Christian schools might operate. In effect, the legislation defined the compelling interests of the state in the lives of children in terms of education.

During this period, private Christian school enrollment flourished. In 2005, the National Center for Educational Statistics (NCES) estimated that 6,073,000 students attended private schools in the United States. Most of these private schools were Christian schools. Of the total enrollment in private Christian schools, 15.2 percent attended conservative Christian schools. Parents enrolled their children in private Christian schools for a number of reasons:

- They removed their children from the public system to avoid the secular humanist philosophy that prevailed within the public system.
- They desired the focus on academics that characterized the private school movement.
- They desired the sheltered atmosphere and the safer conditions that private Christian schools provided.
- They sought a system that would give attention to the moral values and lifestyle taught in the Bible.

During the period that enrollment in private Christian schools and private schools in general was growing, many parents decided to educate their children at home. In December 2008, the National Center for Educational Statistics (NCES) reported that more than 1.5 million American youth—almost three percent of the school-age population—were being home schooled. According to NCES, parents gave the following reasons for choosing to home school their children:

- Concern about the school environment of the public system
- A desire to provide religious or moral instruction
- Dissatisfaction with academic instruction at other schools
- Nontraditional approach to a child's education
- Child has special needs
- Child has a physical or mental health problem

Among those who had been instrumental in the private Christian school movement and the home school movement, this growth seemed to validate the anticipation and excitement expressed years earlier by Paul Kienel, president of the Association of Christian Schools International. "The present-day phenomenon of the Christian school explosion is, in my judgment, one of the great untold stories of our time. . . . It is an inspiring story. . . . Christians are learning that there is a compatible relationship between Christ and education" (1974, p. 9). Famed newscaster and commentator Paul Harvey added, "Christian schools are coming into their own at a time when the truth they represent may very well be the only hope for the next generation" (p. 8).

In the early days of the movement, Robert J. Billings (1978, p. 144) cautioned that Christian schools should not lose sight of their purpose and mission:

> *The Christian school is first a CHRISTIAN school. The spiritual emphasis of the school is of far greater importance than its academic standing in any community. The Christian school should ever keep the spiritual life of the school "red hot." Academic excellence should characterize the Christian school; however, the "heart" of the student is more important than the "head." If the heart is right, the head will be right. Teaching the child to "be" is far more important than teaching the child to "do."*

It is proper to ask this question: Are there elements of significant reform in the Christian school movement? Or, is the movement merely a return to the education model that characterized the public system of the 1950s? Are there elements of significant reform in the home school movement, or is it merely a change of setting? If these movements embody significant reforms, what are those reforms? One might point to the self-paced system of the original Accelerated Christian Education movement (ACE), now called Schools for Tomorrow. Some excellent materials have been published to help teachers incorporate principles of the Word of God into academic subjects. Textbooks have been published that give attention to the truth of Scripture. Also, Bible is being taught as an academic subject in the Christian schools. But does teaching Bible classes make a school Christian? Are we instilling in young people a Christian worldview? Remember the words of Paul: *"And be not conformed to this world: but be ye transformed by the renewing of your mind, that ye may prove what is that good, and acceptable, and perfect, will of God"* (Romans 12:2).

Think about that! Renewing the mind! A mind renewed through the Word of God is transformed in its ability to discern truth from error when presented with the truth claims of this world. Such a mind operates from a foundation composed of the truth claims of the Bible. That's what "worldview" really means—the truth claims one makes to explain life. Is that not what Christian schooling is all about? Rushdoony (1981, p. 3) says,

> *The function of a school is thus to train persons in the ultimate values of a culture. This is inescapably a religious task. Education has always been a religious function of society and closely linked to its religion. When a state takes over the responsibilities for education from the church or from Christian parents, the state has not thereby disowned all religions but simply disestablished Christianity in favor of its own statist religion, usually a form of humanism. An excellent means of analyzing the religion of any culture is to study its concept of education.*

So, what is the purpose of Christian schooling? Can it be any less than the renewing of students' minds to think in terms of the truth claims of the Bible? This doesn't mean that there is no strong commitment to the academics of the curriculum. Excellence in academics should be the standard—after all, such learning is, or should be, an opportunity for young people to learn about the fascinating world God created. But the driving force behind Christian schooling should be to transform the minds of students in the manner described in Romans 12:2 so that they can live in the world without conforming to its standards and values. This means that the students enrolled in

Christian schools should gain a worldview that is consistent with the Word of God.

How well are Christian schools accomplishing this goal right now? One way to determine this is to look at the results of the Worldview PEERS Study (2002). This study examines the results of the PEERS Test, which is produced by the Nehemiah Institute under the leadership of Dan Smithwick. The PEERS study examines the effectiveness of the Christian school movement in teaching a worldview based upon the truth of Scripture. This test examines the worldview of students in five broad categories: politics, economics, education, religion, and social issues.

Although some have questioned the validity of the PEERS Test, it was evaluated for validity and reliability in 1995 during a study directed by Dr. Brian Ray (1995), assisted by a panel of ten experts representing nine states and several regions of the United States. This panel represented both conservative and liberal leanings in terms of the personal worldviews of individual panel members. The panel reached two major conclusions:

1. The validity of the PEERS Test is more than satisfactory for testing and research purposes.
2. Using Cronbach's internal consistency alpha method of analysis, the PEERS Test showed an overall alpha rating of .94, indicating a high level of reliability for the test.

The PEERS Test has been administered to thousands of graduates. Figure 1 shows the results of testing approximately 100, 000 graduates across the United States. It presents a comparison of four major groupings of students over a period of twenty-two years.

Figure 1: PEERS Trend Chart: Worldview Analysis of High School Youth

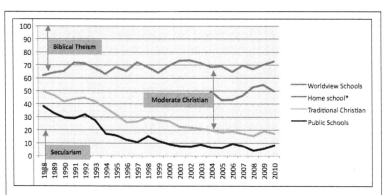

Source: Worldview PEERS Study – AACS, November 2001, by Nehemiah Institute. Used by permission. Data indicates scores on the PEERS Worldview Analysis; first compiled in 2001 and updated annually thereafter.
* Home school data only available beginning 2002

Worldview schools	Christian schools that have made "worldview" a key focus in the school in these particular areas: (1) curriculum selection, (2) faculty training, and (3) parent training. Biblical worldview is not taught as a "class subject" such as English, history, or math, but is the foundation of all classes taught.
Traditional Christian	Standard Christian schools with mainline accrediting agencies such as ACSI, AACS, ACCS, or ACTS. They may or may not have a high school class on the subject of "worldview."
Home school	Majority of school work is being done at home or at home school co-op groups.
Public school	At least 90 percent of students in this category are from Christian homes, attending youth groups in evangelical churches, and attending local public schools. The other 10 percent are actual public school classes (all students in a class) that participated in a PEERS testing session as part of a graduate student research project.

As you can see, Figure 1 does not show a positive picture in terms of how well traditional Christian schools are transmitting a Christian worldview to children. The PEERS Test results show a downward trend in Christian worldview among graduates from traditional Christian schools that parallels the trend among public (secular) schools. Home school graduates hold worldviews that are moderately Christian. By comparison, graduates of schools classified as "worldview schools" in the PEERS study seem to be achieving what should be the purpose of the Christian school movement: graduates of these schools hold a worldview that approaches biblical theism. What distinguishes these schools from traditional Christian schools? They intentionally focus on worldview in curriculum selection, faculty training, and parent training.

Renewing students' minds will require intentional efforts such as these at the school level, where a principal and teaching staff develop or agree on a curriculum that promotes academic and spiritual excellence—and then prepare themselves to deliver that curriculum effectively. It will require a school principal who functions as an instructional and curriculum leader. It will require members of faculty who work collaboratively and collectively to help students graduate with a perspective based on the truth claims of the Bible.

Concerns for Christian educators:

Solomon said, "A wise man will hear, and will increase learning; a man of understanding shall attain unto wise counsels." What can we "hear" or learn from the education research conducted over the past half century? How can it increase our understanding of what works and doesn't work? What wise counsel is available to those seeking to transform the Christian school movement?

First, it seems clear that meaningful and lasting improvement in education cannot be achieved merely by raising goals and expectations. Neither can improvement be accomplished by promulgating directives and regulations from sites distant from the place where education actually occurs—the local school and the professional educators that staff the school. The factory model of administration and leadership that has characterized the secular system of education has failed to produce satisfactory results. The locus for improving the quality of Christian schooling must become the schools themselves—meaning each and every Christian school across the United States—and it must include the school principal and the teaching faculty in the exciting and collaborative work of building a quality Christian school program for the students in their school.

Second, we've learned that giving local schools the authority and responsibility to "make change happen" is not enough to ensure success. School administrators and teachers additionally need ongoing training and professional development (a continual renewal of their minds) to enable them to do the very real and challenging work of school transformation. Most educators haven't been trained to change a school's culture or to harness the power of a learning community to help one another achieve the school's mission, yet such actions are essential to school transformation. These new skills and expectations for educators will require a shift in the way we prepare, develop, and support administrators and teachers.

Third, research suggests that traditional Christian schools are weak in the area where they should be strong: conveying to students a worldview or lifeview that is based upon the truth of Scripture. *This is a weakness that must be addressed.* After all, promoting the acquisition of a biblical worldview is the very reason Christian schools exist. Professional educators serving in the Christian school ministry have a moral obligation to teach a worldview based upon the Bible and to provide a viable, guaranteed curriculum that supports that worldview. If that goal is not achieved, the Christian school movement fails.

There is but one standard for Christian schooling—excellence. Excellence can't be mandated, but it can be fostered, encouraged, nurtured, supported, celebrated, and continually sought after. The trait of reaching for the highest possible achievement can be embodied in the spirit of a school community through the synergistic efforts of school leaders, faculty, and parents. It is through their joint efforts that excellence will be exemplified and instilled in young people as a goal worthy of pursuit.

Imagine being part of a school ministry that is totally dedicated to both student and adult learning. Imagine being part of a school team that's "on a mission" to offer a curriculum that will enable each student and staff member to succeed as learners and as truth-seekers. That's what a learning community is. This type of community conforms to the pattern set forth in 1 Corinthians 12, where Paul describes the interdependence and dedication of the body of Christ, working together to accomplish spiritual purposes. It's a model that taps individual gifts and abilities for the collective good. It's a model for transforming the Christian school movement, supported by the Bible and by the best available education research. But how do we put this model into action?

Part of the answer lies in "systems thinking." Paul didn't use that term when he described the Christian community as the body of Christ, with all of the parts working together to create something more than the sum of its parts. Yet it's exactly the kind of thinking he exhibited when he came up with that particular metaphor. It's a mode of thought that Christian educators will need to develop as we unite to pursue excellence in our schools.

CHAPTER 3

Professional Learning Communities as Vehicles of Systemic Change

Two are better than one; because they have a good reward for their labour... a threefold cord is not easily broken.

King Solomon, Ecclesiastes 4:9, 12b

*If you intend to introduce change that is compatible with the organization's culture, you have only three choices: modify the change to be more in line with the existing culture, alter the culture to be more in line with the proposed change, **or prepare to fail.** (Emphasis added)*

Salisbury and Conner (1994, p. 17)

He is in the way of life that keepeth instruction: but he that refuseth reproof erreth.

Solomon, Proverbs 10:17

From whom the whole body fitly joined together and compacted by that which every joint supplieth, according to the effectual working in the measure of every part, maketh increase of the body unto the edifying of itself in love.

Apostle Paul, Ephesians 4:16

IN *THE FIFTH DISCIPLINE*, CONSIDERED by many to be the classic work on systems thinking, Peter Senge (1990) acknowledges the complexity of change and explains why *systems thinking* is so valuable to anyone wishing to bring about change. As you read his explanation of systems thinking, consider its application to the endeavor of Christian schooling:

Business and other endeavors are . . . systems. They . . . are bound by invisible fabrics of interrelated actions, which often take years to fully play out their effects on each other. Since we are part of that lacework ourselves, it's doubly hard to see the whole pattern of change. Instead, we tend to focus on snapshots of isolated parts of the system, and wonder why our deepest problems never seem to get solved. Systems thinking is a conceptual framework, a body of knowledge and tools that has been developed over the past fifty years, to make the full patterns clearer, and to help us see how to change them effectively.

The Power of Systems Thinking

Senge refers to systems thinking as "the fifth discipline" because it integrates all other disciplines that are essential to bringing about change, fusing them into a body of theory and practice. It is a reminder that the whole can exceed the sum of its parts. That is synergy. That is something to strive for in any educational endeavor.

As a conceptual framework, systems thinking can help us examine Christian schooling as a whole by helping us see the interrelationships among its parts. It is a search for patterns rather than "snapshots" in time. It can help us focus on people (e.g., leaders, teachers, and students) rather than things (e.g., the latest fad or "silver bullet") as the best resource for improving the system.

Think of the Christian school system as a web of relationships among pastors, administrators, teachers, parents, and students. Now expand that web to include those who train teachers and leaders in colleges of education and those who work in various organizations that administer or support Christian schooling. Within this web of relationships, any one person or organization can attempt to make changes. However, those efforts are often designed to answer questions such as *How can I get others to do things my way?* or *How can I put out this fire?* Systems thinking leads us to ask better questions, such as *Which changes within this web would make the most lasting and meaningful difference for the greatest number of people?* Better questions, in turn, will lead to better answers.

The Power of Synergy

Consider what might happen if all the people within the network or "web" of Christian schooling agreed to work together to ask—and seek answers to—better questions. What if we laid aside the petty turf battles that often characterize efforts to improve the educational "product"? What if we agreed to place on the table for examination all our existing ideas about the education of children? What if we also placed on the table the Word of God pertaining to how we as His followers should approach this sacred trust?

When people work together, their efforts are multiplied. When they work together with God, their efforts are magnified. As Solomon wisely counseled, "Two are better than one; because they have a good reward for their labour . . . a threefold cord is not easily broken" (Ecclesiastes 4:9, 12b). The modern word for the dynamic Solomon describes is *synergy*. Synergy is the interaction between two or more agents or forces so that their combined effect is greater than the sum of their individual efforts.

The word *synergy* is frequently used in Christian circles. Synergy is attained when those involved in the work of God get together to discuss and make critical program decisions to revitalize a ministry—for example, the ministry of educating children. Be assured that the matter of educating children is given much attention in the Word of God, especially in the book of Proverbs. Persons involved in this ministry should be concerned about synergy. It is much more than getting together—it is agreeing to the definitions that will apply to the Christian schooling of children. It's working together to multiply efforts for a worthy cause and letting God magnify the results.

The Power of Community

Senge proposes that the question of how to make meaningful changes in a complex system is not a question that should be answered by one person. It's a question that should be asked and answered by a community of people. The word *community* begins with the prefix *com*, which means "with" or "together." The root of the word is *unity*. Therefore *community* speaks of a joint effort, shared meanings, and unity of purpose. In the case of Christian schooling, the shared purpose is to help children grow mentally, spiritually, and otherwise in an educational setting embedded with Christian ideals and values.

Improved learning and growth among students enrolled in Christian schools will take root when board members, pastors, principals, and teaching faculty engage in the challenging but exciting work of defining the Christian school, its mission, its purpose, its values, its goals, and the means to be adopted to achieve those goals.

The work of putting ideas into action, testing them, measuring results, making adjustments, refining definitions, adopting new strategies, and so forth is demanding and often messy. For this reason, it is best accomplished within a community where individuals within the system can support and learn from one another. Senge speaks of a "learning community" or "learning organization" as a group of individuals collectively committed to improving their capacity to produce the desired results. He offers this definition of a learning organization:

> *It is an organization that is continually expanding its capacity to create. It is generative in nature, possessing the power to come up with new ideas, new approaches to solve problems. It demands the abandonment of ingrained constructs, concepts, or practices that do not work. It must be characterized by faith in and respect for the people around you and their ability to think and to generate new ideas.*

The vision of schools as learning communities is a stark contrast to the factory model of schooling that has dominated education for the past few decades. Where the factory model speaks of uniformity, standardization, and bureaucracy, the learning community speaks of collaboration and transformation. Where the factory model speaks of decisions about education flowing from top to bottom, the learning community speaks of decisions flowing from synergistic efforts within a supportive environment. You might say that the factory model, with its numerous rules and hierarchies, represents an "Old Testament" approach to improving education, while learning communities, which emphasize principles and relationships, represent a "New Testament" approach.

We as Christian educators need to pay attention to sound principles and relationships. An examination of the school reform efforts of the past several years tells us we have not yet learned to focus on what goes on at the school building level. We haven't paid enough attention to building synergy within Christian schools and across the organizations that support those schools. Many schools and other organizations have written mission statements, framed them, and proudly hung them on office walls. But most schools don't base daily decisions and actions on a dynamic shared vision for the education of children. Neither secular nor Christian schools have truly harnessed the capabilities of experienced teachers, or examined ingrained concepts about how things are done, or created viable structures for doing so. Ideally, those involved in Christian schools should share a commitment to the children they serve, viewing them as God views them. The governance structure of the school should support them in this endeavor. Instead, many decisions about education are based on unexamined assumptions.

If the philosophers are correct in saying the unexamined life is not worth living, one might extrapolate that the unexamined school is not worth attending. Why? Because in such schools, decisions are not made by people—they're made by default. In such schools, educators are not preparing the next generation for lives of productive service—instead, they're just "having school."

How do we turn off the autopilot and reset our course? Those who have studied the U.S. education system and worked to improve it offer food for thought:

Goodlad (1975) maintains that the optimal unit for educational change is the single school with its pupils, teachers, and principal—those who live there every day—as primary participants. To bring about the transformation that is needed, each school must become a learning organization dedicated to accomplishing God's purposes through education. Dufour and Eaker (1998) use the following terms when applying the learning community concept to a school:

> **Shared Mission, Vision, and Values:** *This involves a collective commitment on the part of a total school staff that communicates to others the belief system of the school and what the staff seeks to create. In the literature, it may also be identified as the moral purpose or mission of the school.*
> **Collective Inquiry:** *The leadership and teaching faculty of the school must become adept at asking the "why" question within a non-threatening atmosphere. Problems are recognized and accepted as the challenge they are, and there is a collective effort to correct them.*

Collaborative Teams: *The staff of a learning community is organized into a number of learning teams. Building a school's capacity to learn, to achieve the goals, is a collaborative rather than individual task.*

Action Orientation and Experimentation: *Learning occurs within the context of taking action, doing something to improve the functioning of the school.*

Continuous Improvement: *Within a learning community, there is uneasiness with just maintaining the status quo. Questioning is something to be desired. The spirit of inquiry is present.*

Results Orientation: *People working within a learning community seek results that can be sustained within a transformed school culture.*

Newmann and Wehlage (1995) say that a learning community must be characterized by three general features:

- Teachers pursue a clear, shared purpose for all students' learning.
- Teachers engage in collaborative activity to achieve that purpose.
- Teachers take collective responsibility for students learning.

Thomas J. Sergiovanni (1995) talks about schools as collections of people rather than organizations. In his works, the term "community" is a metaphor that is prominently used to describe the staff of a school, including the highest-level administrator. For Christian schooling and a Christian school, that would begin with a church pastor or a board of education. It would also include the teaching faculty and certainly the parents of the students enrolled.

Linda Darling-Hammond (1996), writing in *Phi Delta Kappan*, "recommends that schools be structured to become genuine learning organizations for both students and teachers; organizations that respect learning, honor teaching, and teach for understanding." Michael Fullan (2001), the recognized master of educational change concepts, says "changes in beliefs and understandings are the foundation for achieving lasting reform." Newmann and Wehlage (1998) pick up on the same idea: "If schools want to enhance their organizational capacity to boost student learning, they should work on building a professional community that is characterized by shared purpose, collaborative activities, and collective responsibility among staff."

Although Senge uses the terms *community* and *organization* interchangeably, the practices that characterize organizations often do not fit with a definition of community. Communities are concerned with relationships and connections. It is purpose, vision, and passion for some goal that holds communities together. Connections are based on commitment, not contracts. Communities create social structures that unify people and bind them to a set of shared values and ideas.

DuFour and Marzano (2011) use the term *professional learning community* and describe it as a process rather than a program:

> *A professional learning community is an ongoing process in which educators work collaboratively in recurring cycles of collective inquiry and action research to achieve better results for the students they serve. It is not a program to be purchased; it is a process to be pursued but never quite perfected. It is not an appendage to existing structures and cultures; it profoundly impacts structure and culture. It is not a meeting; it is "an ethos that infuses every single aspect of a school's operation." It does not demand that educators work harder at what they traditionally have done; it calls upon all educators—teachers, counselors, and principals—to redefine their roles and do differently.*

Regardless of the terminology used, the principle of a learning community is not foreign to the Word of God. Systems thinking demands that a school be viewed in terms of its interrelationships, its interdependencies, among students, teachers, and administrators. It demands a mutual agreement upon mission, values, and vision. It demands positive relationships whereby the learning community, as it functions, is providing nourishment and support for itself. Again, that is synergy. The whole is greater than the sum of its parts. In other words, the learning community must nourish itself. But that is the nature of the body of Christ.

The Power of Culture

For better or worse, every community and every organization has its own culture—a composite of the ideas, customs, skills, arts, and truth claims of a people. For example, some communities welcome outsiders with open arms, while others greet them with suspicion. Some companies stick suggestion boxes in the lunchroom, while others expect employees at the lower end of the pecking order to "stick to their jobs and let the boss do the thinking." Even families have their own cultures, and when two people marry, each person brings to the marriage the beliefs, expectations, and ideals of the cultures that dominated their families of origin. For instance, when the new husband assumes his wife will serve turkey for Christmas (just like his mom always did), but she serves her family's traditional favorite—ham—instead, he may experience a bit of "culture shock." Culture is real, and it cannot be ignored. As pertaining to Christian schools, culture can be defined in this way:

> *Culture consists of the ideas, the customs, the practices, and the belief system of any group of people who are carrying out a ministry of the Lord.*

Every Christian school is characterized by a culture. Each Christian school is a social system. Each Christian school has systemic qualities that form a lacework for carrying out education. Culture is the totality of the belief system that is behind everything that is done. Usually, the particular characteristics of one's culture are so ingrained that they are not even noticed or questioned. Any effort to change the ministry of Christian schooling will require those within the Christian school community to examine the system and its culture.

If our current system of Christian schooling is to be transformed, it will require a re-culturing of the movement as a whole—and a re-culturing of individual schools. Such re-culturing cannot and should not be imposed from the outside; instead, it must come from within. In this sense, reculturing is a "do-it yourselves" project for each school community. Effecting change from within a community demands mutual trust. It demands a safe environment for examining, questioning, and ultimately changing the culture of a school.

Learning communities create a safe, supportive environment for doing this essential work.

Those of us involved in Christian schooling must begin to reform our thinking and begin building learning communities or learning organizations. That is especially true at the school building level. But it is also true for state and national organizations that provide Christian school leadership. Sometimes we fail to create a path, a path to God and things holy and spiritual, that others may follow. Sometimes we assume that there is nothing to be learned.

Solomon counseled otherwise: "He is in the way of life that keepeth instruction: but he that refuseth reproof erreth" (Proverbs 10:17). Professional Christian educators at all levels of the system should be able to model the attitude and behavior expressed in this Scripture. This means having the humility and commitment to learn new things, support others, maintain high expectations, and create environments that encourage innovation and dialogue among education professionals. In short, it means becoming a "path of life" that can lead others toward truth. This is the work of a learning community. Nothing less can be expected of those testifying to having been birthed into the spiritual body of Christ.

In short, it demands a systemic change, building a school culture that welcomes a full examination of existing belief systems and practices, that values highly every student enrolled in the system, and doing this for the benefit of the children enrolled. There is a moral obligation on the part of leaders of public secular education and private Christian schooling to do this.

The Component Technologies of a Changed System

It is one thing to speak of systemic or cultural change among the leadership and the teaching faculty of a school. It is another to grasp the component technologies that are required of a school staff, including the leaders, to build a generative system for improving the quality of education offered to students. The component technologies begin to define the spirit of a learning community. The school community or organization learns and changes only as individuals within the community or organizations learn and change. Thus, individual learning does not guarantee organizational learning. But, without individuals learning, there can be no organizational learning. Synergy will not be achieved. A learning community is composed of individuals, each with his or her own mindset, and each of these individuals must be motivated to achieve a common purpose and common goals. Without that, there can be no learning community.

Michael Fullan (1993, p. 4) says, "The new problem of change... is what would it take to make the educational system a learning organization – expert at dealing with change as a normal part of its work, not just in relation to the latest policy, but as a way of life." Several terminologies can be found in the literature describing the mindset, attitude, or way of thinking that must characterize a school staff and the leadership of that staff. Senge (1990) is a leader is this regard. He and others have defined four attitudes of mind and heart—the first four of five disciplines, with systems thinking being the fifth—that are required for a learning community to be effective in improving the quality of education offered. Professionals within a learning community must understand these disciplines, herein called component technologies. Consider these component technologies that surface in any serious study and review of the literature related to learning communities or learning organizations.

Component Technology #1: Personal Mastery. Senge (1990, p. 141) uses the term "personal mastery" to describe the discipline of personal growth and learning among individuals within the learning community. It speaks of the ability to think creatively about the goals of the learning community, the private Christian school. It speaks of a creative proactive activity rather than merely reacting to a circumstance. Senge (p. 141) describes two underlying movements that support personal mastery:

1. There must be a continual clarifying of what is important to the learning community. This will limit the time spent on problems. It is the task of the leader to do this.
2. There must be a continual learning of ways to see reality more clearly. This means a staff can no longer assume that everything is right. Nor can they defend every action. It demands that they see the brutal facts of the situation.

Collins (2001) says, "You absolutely cannot make a series of good decisions without first confronting the brutal facts." What a learning community wants and what a learning community honestly sees (realities or brutal facts) must be carefully considered, placing them side by side. Seeing them in juxtaposition will generate a "creative tension," forcing individuals to come together to seek resolution. Thus, the essence of personal mastery is learning to generate and sustain that creative tension in our lives. It demands a continual learning mode on the part of individuals within the learning community, including teachers and the principal.

Component Technology #2: Mental Models. What keeps a school staff from carefully examining new ideas and new approaches? According to Senge (1990), "New insights fail to get put into practice because they conflict with deeply held internal images that limit us to familiar ways of thinking and acting." It is quite natural for one to cling to the mental images or models learned over time. You have probably heard this expression: *It is difficult to teach a person something if they already know everything.* Mindset is just that—a set pattern or way of thinking. Mental models determine how we see the world and how we react to it. Thus, one of the component technologies of a learning community is the ability to open the mental models we possess for examination and discard them if the learning community creates something more promising. A learning community staff must be willing to examine new images and new models for solving problems. New models must be allowed to surface, they must be tested, and they must be examined as possible breakthroughs.

Mental models are frequently tacit, below the surface, and often unseen and unstated or even below the level of awareness. Until a school staff is willing to examine the mental models brought to a planning session, there will be no generative spirit among them. School principals must be able to examine their own mental models and develop ways to inquire into their own and others' ways of thinking. Otherwise, there will be no real collaboration and experimentation among the individuals in the learning community.

Component Technology #3: Shared Vision. Dufour and Eaker (1998) refer to shared vision as "the sine qua non of a learning community." Shared understandings and common values are absolutely essential. Individuals within the body of Christ, and the teaching faculty and leadership of a Christian school, must be able to define a shared vision for the school. **It**

is a common caring. It is a passion within the hearts of people to carry out a work of the Lord, in this case, the education of youth. Within a learning community, it is important that this vision, this caring, become a shared unction and a shared caring, common to all involved in the ministry. Such a vision will serve to unite people; it will grow a respect for each other.

Senge (1990) says that this shared vision will change relationships among those involved in a ministry. It will promote harmony. It is the first step in allowing people who once mistrusted each other to work together and do that on the basis of trust. It will create a common identity for a Christian school staff.

Component Technology #4: Team Learning. Senge (1990) presents the theory and method of *dialogue,* defined as the action of a group, the learning community, becoming open to the flow of a larger intelligence or other ideas. Dialogue, in this case, is a group, a learning community, accessing a pool of common meaning. The purpose of dialogue is to go beyond any one individual's understanding. In dialogue, individuals gain insights that simply could not be achieved individually. The great advantage accruing to Christian people is the fact that God has given His perfect Word that can be brought to the surface as a Christian school staff dialogues concerning issues facing the school. Dialoguing, and time to dialogue, is vital to a learning community.

Dufour and Eaker (1998, p. 25-29) offer numerous ways in which the teaching staff of a learning community can dialogue:

1. Collective inquiry as the engine of improvement, growth, and renewal.
2. Collaborative teams as the basic structure of the learning community, teams addressing perceived facts and issues to promote learning.
3. Action orientation and experimentation as the means of turning aspirations into action and vision into reality.

4. Continuous improvement in responding to the "creative tension" growing from seeing the vision and the brutal facts in juxtaposition.

Culture is a factor in dialogue and team learning among those involved in operating a Christian school. This team includes the pastor, the board of the school, the school principal, the teaching staff of the school, and the parents of the children served by the school. The task of building a learning community for a school involves re-culturing among these people. Remember, such re-culturing should be done *by* members of the learning community, not done *to* them. But they may need help in gaining the skills to make this change.

The Complexity of Systemic Change

Infusing new life into a Christian school is not an easy task. It is very complex. One should never assume that it is something that can be done overnight. After reviewing a number of school improvement efforts, Elmore (1995, p. 11) offered the following comment:

> *We can produce examples of how educational practice could look different, but we can produce few, if any, examples of large numbers of teachers engaging in these practices in large scale institutions designed to deliver education to most children.*

Systemic change is always difficult and complex. Why? Because it involves people, and change is difficult for most people. One salient message in the literature dealing with change is this—*there is a great underestimation of what change is and the factors and processes that account for it.*

Change may be voluntary or imposed. Marris (cited in Fullan, 2001) maintains that all change involves loss, anxiety, and struggle. When leaders fail to recognize this phenomenon as something to be expected, as a natural response, or as something inevitable in a social system, there is a great tendency to misinterpret the action of those who struggle. Marris maintains that people initially react to new experiences in terms of some familiar and reliable construction of what is real. People within a learning community must be able to attach personal meaning to something new, regardless of how meaningful that which is new might be to others.

People will need help in placing a new idea or approach within the context of the truth of Scripture. Understanding precedes acceptance. This means that no innovation can be fully implemented in a Christian school until its meaning is shared. The reader is challenged to think through what this demands of a school principal seeking to transform a school into a learning community. There are two critical things for the principal to know and act upon: the first is that the anxiety and struggle among staff in responding to change must not be viewed as an impediment to growth; and second, the anxiety and struggle resulting from proposed change must be considered by the principal as he or she decides upon action as a proposal for change moves forward.

Again, Marris (cited in Fullan, 2001) addresses this particular issue and urges change agents to exercise patience and compassion for those who don't immediately embrace their ideas:

> *When those who have power to manipulate changes act as if they have only to explain, and when their explanations are not at once accepted, shrug off opposition as ignorance or prejudice, they express a profound contempt for the meaning of lives other than their own. For the reformers have already assimilated these changes to their purposes, and worked out a reformulation that makes sense to them, perhaps through months or years of analysis and debate. If they deny others the chance to do the same, they treat them as puppets dangling by the threads of their own perceptions.*

Even a casual observer of fundamental and evangelical ministries knows that there is much controversy and much disagreement at the beginning of the twenty-first century. Some of the controversy and disagreement can be explained as variance in interpreting biblical truth. That will always be the case. But, perhaps most of it results from a failure to understand that people involved in ministry quickly become a social system or a culture. When changes are imposed upon that system, there results a very natural struggle with the change, because the people impacted will always fall back upon what they know and what makes sense to them. This is not a criticism of teachers and administrators, but it is an indictment of the way in which changes in philosophy and practice are introduced. Why? Because there has not been provided an opportunity for deeper questioning and sustained learning to occur. And, in a Christian ministry, the scriptural basis for the modification is often not established. While a sense of loss and anxiety will always result from changes within a learning community, the sense of loss and anxiety can be significantly diminished with wise and mature planning for change on the part of leadership. A second result is that meaningful reform or change escapes the typical teacher, only to be replaced by superficial, episodic reform that only complicates the problem for everyone.

Schon (1971) addresses this issue with this statement: All real change involves "passing through the zones of uncertainty...the situation of being at sea, of being lost, of confronting more information than one can handle." The wise leader will be aware of the complexity of change and how to work with a staff in accepting and implementing change that may be very desirable. Schon (1971) goes on to say, "The power of social systems over individuals becomes understandable, I think, only if we see that social systems provide... a framework of theory, values, and related technology which enables individuals to make sense of their lives. Threats to the social system threaten this framework."

What Evidence Will Show that Change Has Occurred?

The answer to this question is quite simple: when proposed changes become part of the school culture and when these changes become part of the practice of the faculty and principal. But that is an oversimplification. Fullan (2001) makes these two points: first, change will always fail until some way of developing infrastructures and processes that engage teachers in developing new understandings is found and adopted; and, second, when those involved understand that this is not surface meaning, but deeper meaning about new approaches to teaching and learning. So, change does not come easily given the setting of existing cultures and conditions. But it can be accomplished.

From the perspective of teachers, change and innovation are multidimensional. Innovation involves the possible use of new curricular materials or new technologies; it involves the possible use of new teaching approaches, strategies, or activities; and it invariably involves an alteration of the belief system of a teaching faculty relative to assumptions and theories about education and children. For the teacher in a Christian school, it involves spelling out the values found in the Bible for children, for knowledge, for learning. It involves shaping and transforming the minds of children as stated in Romans 12:2.

So, when has changed occurred? It has occurred when there are changes in beliefs and understandings on the part of teachers and principals. It has occurred when the new conceptions and beliefs are put into practice and have become a part of a re-cultured school, shared by everyone who is a part of this new culture. It has occurred when there is a commitment to revisit these new conceptions and beliefs on a regular basis to confirm them in light of experience and practice. Admittedly, this is quite a challenge to all concerned. The question becomes: Who will lead the charge, and how?

Chapter 4

Guiding Principles of Biblical Leadership

*...To this end was I born, and for this cause came I into the world, **that I should bear witness unto the truth.***

Jesus, John 18:37

But Jesus called them unto Him, and said, Ye know that the princes of the Gentiles exercise dominion over them, and they that are great exercise authority upon them. But it shall not be so among you: but whosoever will be great among you, let him be your minister.

Jesus, Matthew 20:25-26

DO AN ONLINE SEARCH OF the word *leadership* and you will be inundated with definitions, traits, qualities, quotes, and comments about the importance of leadership in any endeavor, whether it involves business, education, or ministry. There seems to be general agreement that the oft-repeated saying is true: "Everything rises or falls on leadership." With that in mind, let's take a few minutes to consider how education leaders are prepared and chosen for their important work.

In the public school system, principals and superintendents are recruited almost exclusively from the ranks of practice. Thus, an individual does not generally get to lead a school or district without having been socialized to its norms, values, predispositions, and routines. This means education leaders are creatures of the organizations they lead. Chances are, their administrative training and experiences have prepared them to uphold the organization's existing norms, values, and routines—all of which, in turn, support the factory model of schooling.

To ask a person selected in this way to critique and transform the very system that has propelled him or her to a leadership position is unfair—and unrealistic. It's asking those in administrative positions to do something they have not been trained or prepared to do. Yet that is what policymakers and education stakeholders often expect of them. Yes, a few gifted and visionary leaders have surfaced since the 1983 publication of *A Nation at Risk*—men and women whose actions have brought about significant changes. But have their actions been inspired or supported by the education system or by innovative leadership training programs? Probably not, or there would be a greater abundance of transformational leaders at work in the public schools.

The same is true of Christian schooling. Its leaders, in most cases, have been prepared to *perpetuate* the system they inherited—not to *question* its assumptions or *transform* its culture. Currently, there is no requirement that principals of Christian schools understand how to develop their staff's capacity for breathing life into a collectively articulated vision of excellence in Christian schooling.

Yet Richard Elmore (2000), who has studied education leadership extensively, views the role of the building principal as the "cause" behind progress (or lack of progress) within a school. He defines the principal's role as one of building capacity rather than maintaining the status quo:

The job of administrative leaders is primarily about enhancing the skills and knowledge of people within the organization, creating a common culture of expectations around the use of those skills and knowledge, holding the various pieces of the organization together in a productive relationship with each other, and holding individuals accountable for their contributions to the collective result.

This definition of leadership says that leaders must be about the business of systemic change—making sure all the parts are working together to achieve a common purpose. It implies a balance of support and accountability as school leaders expand the school's capacity to address complex problems and achieve worthy goals. This approach to leading schools mirrors the biblical approach to leading members of the body of Christ to act with unity of purpose.

Newmann, King, and Young (2000) define *school capacity* as a combination of five elements: (1) teachers' knowledge, skills, and dispositions; (2) professional community; (3) program coherence; (4) technical resources; and (5) principal leadership. Individual growth alone is not enough to improve school capacity. Rather, growth occurs when individuals build new relationships based on authenticity and care, discover new understandings together, and strategize to secure or create the resources needed to offer a viable education program and to make that program coherent. Students and teachers will benefit when the principal of a school understands the various elements of school capacity and becomes expert in applying them within the dynamic system of that school.

Lambert (cited in Sergiovanni, 1992) asserts that school capacity increases when school leaders recognize that "leadership belongs to everyone" and that the school administrator's role "is to cultivate the leadership potential of every single employee, student, and parent in the school system." She further says that leadership is an attitude that informs behavior rather than a set of discrete skills or qualities, whether innate or acquired.

What attitudes should inform the behavior of leaders in Christian schools? Attitudes based on the Word of God are embodied in two biblical principles of leadership:

LEADERSHIP PRINCIPLE #1: **Leaders are servants. (See Matthew 20:25-28)**

In preparing his disciples to carry out the ministry after he has left the earth, Jesus provides profound insight into what it means to be a divinely inspired leader. He says the self-serving, self-promoting, self-glorying ways of the world, and the politicizing of spiritual issues, are the very antithesis of leadership within the body of Christ. He counsels his leaders-in-training to view leadership, instead, as an opportunity to serve and minister to others. His counsel literally turns the worldly view of leadership on its head.

The world's view of leadership positions might be pictured as a pyramid, where "greatness" is equated with the person at the top—with the implication being that those positioned nearer the bottom of the pyramid are of lesser value. For those ministering within the body of Christ, however, the pyramid is to be inverted, with the leader at the "bottom" acknowledging and supporting the great worth and potential of every soul within the pyramid, regardless of position. As Jesus said, "The Son of man came not to be ministered unto, but to minister." He exemplified the attitude and principle of servant leadership.

This principle of **servant leadership** is found in a number of biblical passages. For example, in Luke 14:11, Jesus states, "For whosoever exalteth himself shall be abased; and he that humbleth himself shall be exalted." He then gives a practical application of this principle in a common situation—issuing or accepting a dinner invitation. He challenges his dinner host to take a look at his dinner guest list and to consider his motivations for deciding who "makes it" to the list. Does it include only people of high social rank, or does it also include the hungry widow? He then challenges his disciples to recall times they have been invited to dinner, and to consider how they decide where to sit, once they arrive, in relation to other dinner guests. Will they select the choicest seats for themselves, or will they reserve those seats for the comfort of others? In each case, the Lord challenges people to examine how they view other people—whether it is with contempt or with honor.

What is Jesus teaching His disciples? To say that this passage is often misunderstood and misapplied is an understatement. First, He is not teaching that a position of authority for leaders is not to be desired. That would contradict what Paul teaches in 1 Timothy 3:1: "This is a true saying, If a man desire the office of a bishop, he desireth a good thing." Paul says this is a trustworthy statement. It is a good thing for one to desire the office of bishop, overseer, or elder (assuming one desires the office as an opportunity to serve, of course).

Who is to lead the effort to revitalize the Christian school movement? It is the man or woman who understands the biblical concept of servant leadership, the one willing to stand abreast with classroom teachers as issues of learning are studied. It is the one who chooses to focus on what happens in classrooms and to honor and respect those faced with classroom decisions. It is the one who highly values those individuals who have committed themselves to educating children. It is the one who is willing to serve teachers by supporting them as both learners and teachers (hearers and doers) and by enlarging their capacities for individual and collective leadership within the school.

This principle of servant leadership is affirmed throughout the New Testament. For example, Paul says in Philippians 2:3-4, "In lowliness of mind, let each esteem other better than themselves. Look not every man on his own things, but every man also on the things of others." A review of the current literature about business and education leadership shows that the secular world has embraced the biblical idea of servant leadership. For example, David Pottruck, president and co-CEO of Schwab, observes that Charles Schwab could speak for hours about opportunities to serve others and to thereby make a great difference, and never once speak of profits. Pottruck lists four reasons why Charles Schwab emphasized the principle of service in meetings where he addressed the "culture" of the organization he directed. These four reasons apply not only to business but also to Christian schooling. For example:

- *The principle of service grounds people in something that is unchanging.* Those working in ministry have every reason to expect the stability provided by this kind of direction.
- *It builds a basis for alignment – a single direction toward which to move.* Those ministering or those working in a movement respect this kind of clarity.
- *It serves as a filter for determining who is "with us," and who is not.* Collins (2001) speaks about the need to "have the right people on the bus". We need to have the right people working in Christian schooling—those dedicated to its purpose and to those they serve.
- *It helps export company values to customers.* In a Christian school setting, the principle of service promotes harmony and coherence among those teaching and learning there.

It is interesting to note that Schwab uses the word *culture* in describing his company and references an article titled "New World, Old Traditions," published in 2000. The "old tradition" referenced in the article is the principle of leadership as revealed in the Word of God, recently discovered anew by the business world and used prominently in its current literature. The question is this: If the world of business and industry is discovering great leadership principles in the Word of God, shouldn't we as Christian educators be "ahead of the curve" in understanding and applying such principles? If we're "behind the curve"—and the loss of leadership and direction within the Christian school movement suggests this is the case—why do we hesitate to correct our course? It's time for us to put to work in Christian schools the biblical principles of leadership that the world now clamors to comprehend.

The principle of servant leadership is taught in Scripture. It should also be taught in programs designed to prepare leaders for the Christian schooling ministry, and it should be studied and practiced by those in leadership positions. Servant leadership gets at the issue of the relationship between the leader and those being led. It is a necessity for schools and school staffs desiring to build a learning community or learning culture that addresses the needs of children. It is the key to increasing the capacity of a school's staff to focus decisions and actions on the academic and spiritual growth of children. And that is exactly where the focus should be placed.

LEADERSHIP PRINCIPAL #2: **Strong leaders are guided by a moral compass. (See 1 Timothy 6:11 and 2 Timothy 3:17)**

The Apostle Paul, in speaking to young Timothy, calls him a "man of God" (1 Timothy 6:11). The title given to Timothy by Paul—"man of God"— is simple yet powerfully magnificent. Timothy is being reminded that he is God's man. He has been called and equipped for the task given to him, and he is answerable, ultimately, to no other authority but that of God. This title would apply to that man who senses the call of God upon his life to provide leadership in a program designed to bring knowledge to children. That, too, is a magnificent task. Unfortunately, with each passing day, that task seems to be losing its luster and its appeal. But it is still a high calling of God and should be restored to its former position.

Heifetz (1994) maintains that in times of crisis, policymakers tend to look for a charismatic leader, someone who already has the answers, is decisive, and seems to know exactly what to do to address the crisis. In other words, they are generally looking for a quick fix rather than a long-term solution, to settle for a "crisis manager" instead of identifying a true leader. However, most crises don't happen overnight and can't be solved overnight. Indeed, the search for leadership in crisis situations should focus on individuals who understand systems and the complexity of systems. Such individuals can not only steer the ship clear of the iceberg, but can also help the crew learn how to avoid such near-collisions in the future. In the case of Christian schooling, what's needed is someone who shows great strength of conviction for the truth revealed by Jesus Christ, someone who is able lead a staff to search for new ways of solving old problems, someone who embodies the principle of servant leadership.

The second time the expression "man of God" is used in the New Testament is in 2 Timothy 3:17. Here the emphasis is on how the Word of God equips the "man of God" for every good work. This passage, like the first, challenges those in the ministry to couple strong leadership with a moral compass, with righteous living positioned as true north and the leader acting as a "witness of good works" that will lead to righteous living.

The principle of servant leadership does not contradict the principle of strong leadership. Practicing the principle of servant leadership does not make one weak. Was Jesus exhibiting weakness when he washed his disciples' feet? Of course not. It was an act of humility and love—a divine model for the attitude leaders are to have toward those they serve. In performing this act, "the Word was made flesh" in the sense that the spiritual words or teachings of Jesus were made manifest in the world.

Jesus taught and led not only by words, but also by example. Do we have the courage and conviction to follow his lead? Is our moral compass pointing toward the true north of righteous living, or is it pointed toward our own selfish desires for worldly honors? Are we as leaders in Christian schooling bearing witness of the good works that will lead us to righteous living, or are we using flattery or silence to avoid saying what needs to be said and doing what needs to be done?

These questions are not a justification for charging ahead with self-righteous indignation. Rather, they are an invitation to reflect on the best way to bring about lasting change within a complex system. Just as being a servant leader doesn't mean being weak, being a strong leader doesn't mean being a tyrant. Functioning as a servant leader means honoring, respecting, and supporting those who work directly with children. Administration exists to support teaching and learning in a school.

Functioning as a strong school leader means helping everyone in the system view education as a means for moving toward the true north of righteous living. It requires continual course corrections—not by forcing one's own ideas on others, but by inspiring teachers through words and deeds to work together and to support one another as they strive for excellence in the school's classrooms, hallways, and playgrounds. It means seeking after the insights, strategies, and the theories of knowledge and learning that are appropriate for the Christian school movement, and working with others to make those things manifest in Christian schools.

Christian schools needs strong leaders who understand how to *manage things* (facilities and resources) and *lead people* within the context and culture of a particular school setting. These leaders need to be knowledgeable about education and schooling. They need to understand and use the component technologies of systemic change to achieve desired results. They need to be able to support the development of a professional learning community that will increase the school's capacity to educate children. Children and learning must be restored to the focus or center of Christian schools.

These are tall orders for those dedicated to carrying out a vital function within the body of Christ—that of preparing the next generation for lives of productive service. The ministry of Christian schooling demands a common and shared effort to bring about this transformation by people who claim a relationship with the Lord Jesus Christ. In executing this responsibility, let's not forget to look to Scripture for guidance and examples. Just as Jesus went to great lengths to build leadership capacity among his "staff" of disciples, and Paul later emphasized the need for unity among all members of the church, those involved in Christian schooling can harness the power of righteous leadership and unity to bring forth good fruits.

The Christian School Movement Is Blessed with Truth

One of the greatest truths of Scripture is found in John 18:37. Jesus is speaking to Pilate the night before the crucifixion. Pilate asks, "Art thou a king then?" Jesus responds by stating clearly His reason for coming into the world: **to bear witness to or to establish truth.** Think of that! Everything that He did is embodied in that truth. All that pertains unto life and godliness is embodied in that truth. This means knowledge about the proper education of children in a Christian school setting is embodied in that truth. The responsibility of parents for the education provided to children is embodied in that truth. The responsibility of the older generation to the younger generation is embodied in that truth. The teaching/ learning function of the church is embodied in that truth. The importance of knowledge as the basis for conscience and development of conviction is found in that truth. What an amazing revelation! It is astounding to the soul of one meditating upon those thoughts.

In practical terms (for all spiritual truths have practical applications), this means we are not left to our own devices in our search for sound leadership principles. We don't have to start from scratch to figure out how to lead the Christian school movement to higher ground. We can look to the Bible, and to the life and teachings of Jesus Christ in particular, for answers about how to lead, how to teach, and how to treat one another. The leadership principles discussed in this chapter are but two examples of the truths available in Scripture. Additional insights are available to anyone in the education ministry who seeks the blessing of truth.

CHAPTER 5

Dimensions of Leadership in Christian Schooling

*And they said unto me, The remnant that are left of the captiv-
ity there in the province are in great affliction and reproach: the
wall of Jerusalem also is broken down, and the gates thereof are
burned with fire. And it came to pass when I heard these words,
that I sat down and wept, and mourned certain days and fasted,
and prayed before the God of heaven.*

Nehemiah 1:3-4

*Your position never gives you the right to command. It only
imposes on you the duty of so living your life that others can
receive your orders without being humiliated.*

Dag Hammarskjold

PEOPLE AND SYSTEMS ARE MULTIDIMENSIONAL, and so is leadership. Basing leadership on biblical principles and developing an
understanding of systemic change are vital to the success of leaders seeking to implement and sustain improvements in Christian
schooling. But there's more to it than that.

The multiple dimensions of education leadership have been acknowledged and defined in the research and practice literature. Fullan (2001) discusses "five elements of leadership" that promote balance within a school and provide a framework for building a successful learning community. Sergiovanni (1995) describes "forces of leadership," and Kouzes and Posner (2002) address "five practices of exemplary leadership." These authors, and numerous others, draw on quality research to describe in great detail the nature of leadership needed to support synergy within and among a school's staff. Although the terminology used by these authors varies, the dimensions of leadership that they describe are very similar.

By becoming familiar with the dimensions of leadership, those wishing to create a culture of excellence within Christian schools can greatly improve the likelihood of success. Make no mistake—creating such a culture is an undertaking as monumental as it is worthwhile. Such significant change entails more than adopting new attitudes and practices, and even more than implementation. It requires a change of sufficient magnitude to sustain quality practices over time.

There is a difference between adoption and implementation: Anyone with much experience in education can point to numerous fads that have come and gone—open schools and classrooms, team teaching, and ungraded classrooms, to name just three. These fads were adopted but never fully implemented, and not at all sustained. Likewise, *changes* within a Christian school may be adopted and even implemented, but *transformation* means sustaining the most effective changes by weaving them into the culture or social system of the school. In other words, new attitudes and practices must be *institutionalized*. Miles (1983) says that institutionalization means that change is built into the very life of the school.

Understanding the dimensions of leadership described in this chapter will be helpful to leaders in the Christian school movement at all levels, including pastors, college staff, members of boards of education, principals, and teachers. All are leaders in one way or another. All play an important role in building a Christian school program that prepares students spiritually, mentally, and otherwise to face life in the twenty-first century.

DIMENSION #1: **Adopting and Clarifying a Moral Purpose or Mission**

The moral purpose or mission of a school drives all the decisions and actions of the learning community within that school. It affects all who work in the school and all who attend it. It can have a "ripple effect" on families and on the broader community as well. Dufour and Eaker (1998) say that a school's mission statement answers the question *Why does this school exist?* Bardwick (1996) says the mission statement answers the question *What is the business of our business?* To be effective, a mission statement must be meaningful, succinct, and *alive*—that is, it must inform everything that happens in the school.

What is the relationship between leadership and mission? Sergiovanni (2000) believes that a leader's top priority should be to protect the lifeview that serves as the basis for moral purpose and mission. Sergiovanni uses the term "life-world" to describe the ideas and commitments that function as a source of authority for what people do. Unlike hierarchical authority or legal authority, the authority of one's life-world or lifeview influences both thought and behavior and provides a structure for defining an educational program. For Christian educators who are committed to a lifeview based on the truth of Scripture, Sergiovanni's observation is critical. Most citizens want schools to reflect values and beliefs that are meaningful in their lives. In fact, the Christian school movement was founded upon that principle.

Moral purpose is crucial to the long-term effectiveness of any Christian school. It has two dimensions: a desirable *end* but also the *means for accomplishing that end*. It is the latter that should be a major concern for Christian school leaders. The desirable end for Christian schooling is generally agreed upon by those involved, but the means employed may fail to meet the moral standard. For example, there is often a failure to adequately provide for the needs of the teaching faculty, leading many to say that the teaching faculty is the group making the greatest sacrifice to support a system of Christian schooling. Unfortunately, this is often true, and some educators even brag about their sacrifice. But, does the great sacrifice asked of them, even if made to accomplish a desirable end, meet the standard of the school's moral purpose or mission? When other salaries and benefits in a ministry are sufficient to meet needs, the expectation that the teaching faculty make a greater sacrifice fails to meet the standard of the moral purpose. The expectation that they transform the school and sustain excellence without the training and support needed to do so also fails to meet the standard. Those in leadership positions need to consider the human and professional needs of the school staff, for in addressing those needs, they are also addressing the needs of the children being taught, thus fulfilling the school's moral purpose.

The Bible has many examples of moral purpose. In the book of the Bible that carries his name, Nehemiah made two inquiries while he was in exile in Babylon and serving in the court of Artaxerxes. First, he inquired concerning the people of Jerusalem; second, he inquired about the city itself. When those questions were answered, Nehemiah said, "I sat down and wept, and mourned certain days, and fasted, and prayed before the God of heaven" (Nehemiah 1:4). From that point on, the answers to Nehemiah's two questions shaped the moral purpose for all of his activities. As a result, the wall of the city was rebuilt, and Jerusalem became a fortified city once again. Under Nehemiah's governorship, civil authority was re-established. Worship was re-established, and God's fidelity in restoring His people was demonstrated time and again. Why? Because one man, Nehemiah, adopted a moral purpose, a passion for carrying out a work of the Lord, and he did so in spite of the opposition of Sanballat and Tobiah while maintaining faithfulness to the directions given to him by God Himself. Nothing swayed

Nehemiah from this focus.

Sadly, research suggests that Christian schools often close because of a loss of vision or moral purpose and a loss of effective leadership (Fitzpatrick, 2003). It seems that, somehow, these schools have been swayed from their focus. When one thinks of what Scripture says about the education of children, about the foundational aspect of knowledge in shaping a child's conscience, and the great need for conviction drawn from the truth of Scripture, such loss of focus seems inexcusable. When one sees the conditions that exist in many homes, including Christian homes, one must ask: *Is there not cause for leaders in Christian schooling to rediscover a moral purpose and vision for this ministry?*

Concern for moral purpose or mission is not confined to Christian schooling. Such concern fills secular literature on education leadership. Sergiovanni (1999) states the case in this way:

> *Ask the next five people you meet to list three persons they know, either personally or from history, who they consider to be authentic leaders. Then, have them describe these leaders. Chances are your respondents will mention integrity, reliability, moral excellence, a sense of purpose, firmness of conviction, steadiness, and unique qualities of style and substance that differentiate the leaders they choose from others. Key in this list of characteristics is the importance of substance, distinctive qualities, and moral underpinnings. Authentic leaders anchor their practice in ideas, values, and commitments, exhibit distinctive qualities of style and substance, and can be trusted to be morally diligent in advancing the enterprises they lead. Authentic leaders, in other words, display character, and character is the defining characteristic of authentic leadership.*

Jesus Himself taught that paying attention to the needs of children is a moral obligation. "Suffer the little children to come unto me, and forbid them not; for of such is the kingdom of God," He reminded His disciples (Mark 10:14). "But whoso shall offend one of these little ones which believe in me, it were better for him that a millstone were hanged about his neck, and that he were drowned in the depth of the sea" (Matthew 18:6).

For the sake of the children, adopting and clarifying a moral purpose or mission is a critical dimension of leadership in Christian schools. The process should involve the entire teaching faculty as well as parent representatives and church administrators. Adoption of a mission statement means accepting a well-defined moral purpose for the school and applying it as decisions are made. A strong mission statement sets parameters that help the school define the nature of its program. It enables school leaders and staff to say *yes* to things that support the mission and *no* to things that should not be included in the program.

Senske (2003) states that people crave purpose in their professional lives. Creating a purposeful culture begins by clearly defining the values and vision of an organization. Establishing a purpose-driven school benefits not only the teaching professionals who work there but also the students whose lives they influence on a daily basis. And those precious lives are greatly in need of positive influences from strong Christian role models. Consider this: Ken Ham (2009), in a research effort to determine when and why some 1,000 twenty-somethings left the church, concluded that more than ninety percent of them "checked out" during the elementary and middle school years. What a tremendous loss. It is cause for alarm. The responsibility for engaging children in school and helping them develop a biblical worldview falls to Christian school leaders as they lead their staffs to define "what matters" and to focus on it.

DIMENSION #2: **Understanding the Complexity of Systemic Change**

During the 1970s and 1980s, when Christian schools were opening at the rate of two or three a day, leaders in the Christian school movement did the only thing they knew to do—they modeled the new schools on the public school system. In the literature, this model is often referred to as the "factory model," in part because key decisions about children and education are not made on the front line but in the boardroom (i.e., by a board of education or by church leaders). These decisions were then passed along to principals, and then to teachers.

In those early days of the movement, attention was primarily given, particularly in national and state meetings, to motivating those on the front lines of Christian schooling. This effort created a conundrum: school staff left those meetings highly motivated to *do something*, but they didn't know exactly *what* to do once they returned home. Even when attempts were made to structure meetings around matters of pedagogy and effective school administration, there were few people available to offer that message. Thus, national and state meetings often became "preaching sessions" or pep rallies rather than platforms for delivering practical advice on how to implement an effective program of Christian schooling. Opportunities to address issues of great concern to administrators and teachers were lost, as were opportunities to build schools' capacity to produce positive, lasting results.

School capacity is important. Elmore (1996) says this: "The fundamental unit of accountability should be the school, because that is the organizational unit where teaching and learning actually occurs. Evidence from evaluations of teaching and student performance should be used to improve teaching and learning." It naturally follows that, if improvement in the education of children is to occur, the focus of that effort must be upon the local school building, the administrator of that school, and the teaching faculty of that school. Furthermore, issues of pedagogy and student learning within the context of the school cannot be ignored.

Unfortunately, the organizational structure and culture of most schools, including Christian schools, almost guarantees that teaching and learning are not addressed in a systematic, effectual way. This is partly because most schools' organizational structures are characterized by what Tyack (1979) calls "loose coupling." Loose coupling is "a form of school organization based on a locally centralized school bureaucracy, governed by elected boards, with relatively low status (mostly female) teachers working in relative isolation from each other under the supervision of (mostly male) administrators whose expertise was thought to lie mainly in their mastery of administrative rather than pedagogical skills." Within such an organizational structure, a school becomes a collection of classrooms and individual teachers who have little contact with each other, overseen by a principal who often shields the school and its teachers from outside influences as well. In other words, there is no effort to coordinate or "couple" the efforts of the heart, mind, hands, and feet of the school body, or to energize that body through external ideas and inspiration.

Within any system characterized by loose coupling, says Cuban (1988), "direct involvement in instruction is among the least frequent activities performed by administrators of any kind at any level, and those who do engage in instructional leadership activities on a consistent basis are a relatively small portion of the total administrative force." This administrative model works as a buffer for the teaching staff, protecting them from disruptions—but also from improvements. Because teaching is viewed as isolated work to be protected, instructional improvements can occur only as voluntary acts among consenting adults. There is no organized, collective, collaborative effort to improve teaching practices. This condition describes the administrative system at work in most Christian schools.

Standards-based reform presumes accountability, certainly for the school, and even the classroom. There is the presumption that students should receive instruction in selected subjects and topics. Certainly Christian schools and leaders within the movement are accountable to God, to the parents who pay the tuition bill, and to the students they teach. Yet, loose coupling in a school's administrative structure can prevent the school from fulfilling its responsibilities. With teachers isolated from one another, and administrators generally being chosen on the basis of personal qualities rather than mastery of professional knowledge, opportunities for improvement within the system are limited. The result is the previously mentioned conundrum: the school becomes a warehouse for hard-working, well-intentioned individuals who often lack the knowledge, skills, and relationships they need to continually improve their effectiveness as teachers and leaders.

If school leaders are to change this dynamic, they must develop an understanding of the complexity of systemic change and how to lead such change. They need to know why and how to create a new school culture that *includes* a Scripture-based mission, values, and vision; *involves* the staff in collective inquiry; *harnesses* the power of collaborative teams to creatively attack problems; *encourages* purpose-driven action and experimentation; *develops* a program of continuous improvement; and *emphasizes* the need for positive results.

In short, Christian schools need leaders who are willing to become experts in systemic change. This means school administrators can no longer be chosen solely on the basis of personal qualities, or even on the basis of administrative experience. Rather, there is a demand for school leaders to have or to acquire two kinds of expertise:

1. **Intimate knowledge of teaching and learning.** School leaders must be able to recognize, value, develop, implement, support, and sustain effective teaching practices within and across every classroom in the school.
2. **Deep understanding of systemic change.** School leaders must have knowledge of the change process required to re-culture a Christian school, offering a quality program for students and providing the human, social, technical, and structural resources necessary for the staff to achieve the school's moral purpose.

DIMENSION #3: **Building Relationships within a Learning Community**

Kouzes and Posner (2002) maintain that "leadership is a relationship." It is a relationship among the staff of a school, which includes those who sense a call to lead and those who are willing to follow. Leadership, they write, is an identifiable set of skills and practices that are available to many, not just a charismatic few. Kouzes and Posner reject the "great person" theory of leadership—the idea that leadership skills are reserved for only a few individuals at the top of any organization, business, or school system. Their research declares this thinking to be a myth and provides evidence that the skills and practices of a quality leader can be defined and learned. This means such skills can be addressed in administrative preparation programs and improved with practice. This discovery alone is cause for great hope, because there are many potentially dynamic leaders dedicated to the success of the Christian school movement. These individuals are needed now as never before.

Among the skills needed by today's Christian school leaders is the ability to **build right relationships among the members of a school's staff.** If "right relationships" among a school staff are ever to prevail—relationships that will support a collective and collaborative approach to addressing challenges within the school—surely it should be in a Christian school setting with a staff of Christian teachers, each of whom can bear testimony of a right relationship with Jesus Christ. That means that each of these persons has been saved, having experienced the new nature that comes through a new birth and having become a part of the body of Christ.

There is ample biblical support for Kouzes and Posner's (2002) assertion that "leadership is a relationship." The Apostle Paul addresses the nature of right relationships among a body of believers in 1 Corinthians 12, verses 14-16. There, Paul refutes the argument of one who would say concerning a body of believers, "they don't need me." In verses 20-25, he also refutes the argument of one who might say, "I don't need them." The very nature of the body of Christ is such that it is characterized by interdependencies. One needs the body of Christ, and the body of Christ needs individuals. Paul speaks of the body as "edifying itself in love" (Ephesians 4:16). There should be no loners on the staff of a Christian school. Development of learning communities in Christian schools should be a natural pattern. Recall that the "com" in the word *community* means "with or together," so the very word speaks of association and relationship. It speaks of joint effort and shared meaning on the part of those having immediate contact with children and those who lead and direct that effort. Building relationships within a Christian school staff is much more than sending out a communiqué requesting staff members to be kind and gracious with each other. Relationships, within this context, refer to a total staff functioning together, working collectively and collaboratively, to improve learning. That is synergy. It demands a mutual respect for the skills and expertise of each person on a staff. Kouzes and Posner (1998) have identified seven "essentials" that must be in place if these kinds of relationships are to flourish:

1. Clear standards must be in place, and they must be understood.
2. The expectation that everyone "does his best" is accepted and practiced.
3. Members of the staff have learned to be good listeners.
4. Appropriate recognition is given, and it is personalized.
5. There is a reporting of successes.
6. Successes are celebrated by the entire staff.
7. People take pride in setting high examples for others to follow.

These seven essentials serve as a launching pad for much greater things.

Sergiovanni (1995) carefully defines and contrasts two types of leadership— transactional and transformative. The *transactional leader* essentially trades or exchanges needs and services with his or her followers so that objectives can be achieved. Sergiovanni refers to this as "leadership by bartering," and it can be observed daily as decisions are made in government-run schools and in most Christian schools. It should be viewed as the first stage of leadership development. The *transformative leader,* by contrast, unites with followers in efforts to achieve high-level goals that have been accepted by both leader and followers. Under such leadership, the minds and hearts of individuals within the Christian school ministry become fused to accomplish a common purpose. Transformative leadership is necessary for synergy. It is necessary for building a learning community. It is necessary for structuring the kind of relationships needed in a ministry of education to children. Such leadership ensures that a moral purpose guides all that is done.

Sergiovanni (1995) describes four stages of leadership that contribute to something very desirable—a synergistic relationship among school leaders and those who follow. These stages, as applied to Christian schooling, may be described as follows:

1. **The first stage is leadership by bartering.** At this stage of leadership, the wants and needs of followers and the wants and needs of leaders and policymakers are negotiated until an *agreement* is struck. Most schools are led and administered in this way, particularly with collective bargaining arrangements governing the process in many states. This stage of leadership responds to the physical, social, security, and ego needs of individuals within the schools.

2. **The second stage is leadership by building.** In this stage, the goal is to begin *developing the potential* of the entire staff and building expectations on the part of the leader and the teaching faculty to strive for higher levels of commitment and performance. Transformative school leaders build individual and collective capacity

within the school by engaging its staff in a moral purpose, involving them in significant decisions about the school's educational program, encouraging an environment of collegial support, and creating opportunities for staff members to increase their competence in helping children learn and grow.

3. **The third stage is leadership by bonding.** There is great moral purpose in educating children in a Christian school. Leaders must begin to arouse awareness and consciousness of this moral purpose to the level of a *shared covenant* that will bond the leader and followers in a stronger commitment to achieve goals. Leadership by bonding allows participants to gain great satisfaction in being able to aid in preparing children to become glowing testimonies to the truth of Scripture.

4. **The fourth stage is leadership by binding.** In this stage, the goal of the leader is to make routine the school improvements agreed upon by the total staff, thus conserving staff energy for new initiatives and new projects. Improvements become real only as they become *institutionalized* and are woven into the new culture of the school. The ultimate goal is a school culture that promotes excellence at all levels, in every sense of the word.

A careful study of Sergiovanni's four stages of leadership will reveal that each stage has merit. The leadership-by-bartering stage will lead to improved competence on the part of those involved in a ministry. However, the development of extraordinary commitment and performance may not occur. And, acceptable performance levels may not be sustained without constant monitoring. It is leadership at the last three stages that has potential to encourage people to transcend "acceptable" levels of competence and commit to performance levels that are beyond what leaders might expect. If

Christian schooling is indeed a ministry of and for the Lord, very high levels of commitment and performance should become the norm within a recultured school. Volumes of good research are available to those wishing to examine principles of leadership in greater depth. Those who serve in leadership positions, and those who aspire to such positions, are encouraged to delve more deeply into the literature. (This book's appendices provide a starting point.) Development of right relationships in and among the leaders and followers within a Christian school ministry is paramount to the transformation of Christian schools. Right relationships are essential to the functioning of a strong learning community within the school. Such a learning community is, in turn, vital for transforming culture and practice in Christian schools.

DIMENSION #4: **Creating Solutions and Sharing New Understandings**

Knowledge creation and knowledge sharing are important values within a learning community, and strong leaders know how to facilitate both. The kind of knowledge referred to here is not simply the accumulation of factual information. Accumulating information is no great task in this information age. Brown and Duguid (2000) say, "Information is machines. Knowledge is people. Information becomes knowledge only when it takes on a 'social life.'" Fullan (2001) adds, "By emphasizing the sheer quantity of information, the technocrats have it exactly wrong: if only we can provide greater access to more and more information for more and more individuals, we have it made. Instead, what you get is information glut." It is the responsibility of the leader to help followers make good judgments and choices about what information is important to consider and what can be filtered out.

Fullan (2001) provides helpful insight into the importance of context in helping people apply knowledge:

Focusing on information rather than use is why sending individuals and even teams to external training by itself does not work. Leading in a culture of change does not mean placing changed individuals into unchanged environments. Rather, change leaders work on changing the context, helping create new settings conducive to learning and sharing that learning.

Can a teaching staff and the leadership of a school study the problems facing the school, remove policies and practices that hinder students' learning, and institute new ideas and practices? Of course they can—if the school leader sets the stage for this important work.

Fullan (2001) writes extensively about the research completed by Nonaka and Takeuchi in 1995. In their study of successful Japanese companies, they found that the success of these companies was not due to their use of technology or the wealth of information gained via technological advances; rather, the successful companies they studied were good at organizational knowledge creation. These companies attacked their own problems, created new knowledge and understandings about how to define and solve those problems, and disseminated these new understandings throughout the organization by embodying them in their service delivery systems.

Nonaka and Takeuchi (1995) distinguish between two types of knowledge: *Explicit knowledge* consists of words and numbers that can be communicated in the form of data and information (for example, student achievement in reading often dips in the fourth grade). *Tacit knowledge* consists of skills, beliefs, and understandings that may be below the level of awareness (for example, students need extra help with reading comprehension skills in fourth grade as they transition from "learning to read" to "reading to learn"). This latter kind of knowledge represents a vast reservoir that is often untapped in schools as well as businesses. This knowledge is personal, and it may be hard to formalize. It may be deeply rooted in an individual's experience, worldview, values, and belief system. But it's there. The leader's task is to help people within the organization recognize and articulate tacit understandings so that they can be examined, discussed, practiced, and fine-tuned within the learning community. Christian school leaders should make every effort to tap into the tacit knowledge that exists within the minds and hearts of the school staff. This knowledge has been gained through experience, and bringing it to the surface releases the power of innovation. To put this kind of knowledge to work within the school, leaders must first create the structures, time, and encouragement necessary for staff members to interact with one another as they share and compare tacit knowledge. Von Krogh and colleagues (2000; as cited in Fullan, 2001) use the term "knowledge enabling" to describe the work of facilitating relationships and conversations for the purpose of enabling school staff members to share their personal or tacit knowledge. Such activities can increase staff members' respect and appreciation for one another, thus creating an environment in which creativity can flourish as issues of teaching and learning are addressed. Von Krogh et al. (2000) claim that there is an explicit link between knowledge building on the part of the school staff and the internal commitment that staff is willing to make to enable good things to occur.

Creating solutions and sharing new understandings—here identified as the fourth dimension of leadership—can occur only if the third dimension (building relationships within a learning community) is in place. Creating an atmosphere of trust is essential to this effort. Members of the learning community must feel they can rely on others within the learning community to listen to and respect their ideas. Constructive and helpful relationships encourage people to share their insights and to freely discuss their concerns.

DIMENSION #5: **Building Coherence within the Learning Community**

As discussed earlier, a succinct and purposeful mission statement provides focus and direction to a Christian school ministry. It can also serve as the basis for saying "no" to innovations that do not fit with the moral purpose and mission. Knowing when to say "no" is essential to building coherence within a school's learning community. Why? Because trying to implement too many innovations can result in a school program that is confusing, disconnected, episodic, piecemeal and, as a result, of superficial quality.

The idea of saying "yes" to some things and "no" to others, however, oversimplifies the approach needed to establish program coherence in a living, changing, complex system. And a school system is exactly that. Pascale, Millemann, and Gioja (2000) underscore the complexity of living systems in their description of four principles that characterize them.

1. **In a living system, equilibrium is a precursor to death.** When a living system is in a state of equilibrium, it is less responsive to changes occurring around it, meaning it is in a state of maximum risk. Even the most casual observer can see that the pace of change within our society, especially its departure from principles of truth as found in the Word of God, has quickened greatly in the last quarter century. In this situation, equilibrium within the Christian school movement is not desirable; the ministry must respond to societal changes if it hopes to endure.

2. **In the face of a threat, or when united in the face of a great opportunity, a living system will move toward the edge of chaos.** Equilibrium will be disturbed. Being in that state will evoke high levels of experimentation, and fresh solutions are likely to be found. Individuals within a ministry cooperate and collaborate in dealing with threat.

3. **With the resulting high level of excitement, the living system will tend to reorganize itself.** New forms and practices will emerge from that excitement.

4. **Living systems cannot be directed toward a linear path.** The Christian school movement and Christian schools are nonlinear initiatives. They are dynamic, and unforeseen events and consequences ("disturbances to the system") are inevitable. The challenge for a leader is to disturb the system in a purposeful manner that approximates the desired outcome. For example, as online learning becomes widespread and "disturbs the system" of brick-and-mortar schools, more parents might opt to enroll their children in online classes rather than in Christian schools. An innovative Christian school leader might find a way to harness the power of online learning and "disturb the system" to support the school's moral purpose. For example, imagine what might happen if the school asked each graduating class to collaboratively create a multimedia presentation on important academic lessons that have spiritual applications. Imagine showcasing these presentations on the school's website. This exercise would promote *higher*-level thinking among students, spur insights among students and their audience, and showcase the potential advantages of attending a Christian school.

Fullan (2001) makes the point that a wise leader will gently "nudge" the living system out of its equilibrium with the introduction of new ideas or new approaches. The response of the living system will be one of "self-organizing" to accommodate the new concepts. Pascale et al. (2000) offers this advice to leaders as the living system is nudged: *design more than engineer, discover more than dictate, and decipher more than presuppose.* Fullan (2001) and Pascale et al. (2000) suggest that disturbing the equilibrium of the living system is a good thing. The result of nudging the living system may be the best route to greater all-around coherence.

According to Selznick (1957), a leader is primarily an expert in the promotion and protection of values, of mission, and of purpose. This is no less true within a ministry of Christian schooling than it is elsewhere. Selznick further states that two domains exist side by side in a school. One is a technical-instrumental domain, and the other is a values/moral purpose domain. The first includes methods and means. The latter includes goals, purposes, and values. Both domains are important. Selznick observes that when the values/moral purpose domain is the driving force for what goes on in a school, and the technical-instrumental domain plays a supporting role, the school will be transformed from a run-of-the-mill organization into a vibrant, unique, and generally more effective, generative institution. The values and moral purpose serve as the basis for defining all aspects of the technical-instrumental domain. Only in this way will the ministry become a source of deep meaning and significance. Leaders who allow the technical-instrumental domain to dominate are emphasizing means, not ends.

Any living system will be characterized by a level of "messiness" as the leader nudges the system to deal with new ideas and challenges. Leaders must learn to accept the fact that "messiness" will occur. And it is the means of creating a "buzz" within the system as the staff works on new ideas and new challenges. The school leader must engage the staff in becoming proficient in judging what new ideas and new challenges comport with the values and moral purpose of the Christian school.

The Pace of Progress

Given the many challenges facing Christian schooling today, one might expect that the community of leaders within the movement would be eager to take immediate action. For this to happen, two things must occur:

1. Christian school leaders at all levels must apply biblical principles of leadership and increase their understanding of the five dimensions of leadership discussed in this

chapter as the Christian school movement acknowledges and confronts its challenges head-on.

2. Leaders within the Christian school movement will
need to abandon two lines of thinking. The first is the
tendency to approach issues as battles to protect one's
turf, whether that turf is a state or national organization,
an individual school, or a teacher preparation college.
The second is the tendency to believe that a single type
or level of organization has all the answers for getting
the movement back on a course. This belief is simply
not true. Individuals working at all levels within various
organizations can and should contribute to transforming the system. In fact, transformation cannot occur
unless individuals at all levels of the system buy into
the changes and agree to them by making them part of
their practice.

Progress will be slow, and that fact must be accepted. Claxton
(1997) addresses the issue of the "pace of progress" in his article
"Hare Brain, Tortoise Mind." In the fable of the tortoise and the
hare, the hare is quick, clever, and high on hubris. The tortoise is
slow and purposeful, adapting to the circumstance he is in. The
tortoise wins. The lesson in Claxton's article is this: Haste is not
always the best friend of one who wants to bring progress to a living system. Making progress in a living system such as Christian
schooling requires that changes be made in a slow and deliberate
fashion. Claxton (1997) offers this advice to leaders:

> *When we are trying to decide where to spend our holidays, it*
> *may well be perfectly obvious what the parameters are: how*
> *much we can afford, when we can get away, what kinds of*
> *things we enjoy doing and so on. But when we are not sure*
> *what needs to be taken into account, or even which questions*
> *to pose—or when the issue is too subtle to be captured by the*

familiar categories of conscious thought—we need to recourse to the tortoise mind. If the problem is not whether to go to Turkey or Greece, but how best to manage a difficult group of people at work, or whether to give up being a manager completely and retrain as a teacher, we may be better advised to sit quietly and ponder than to search frantically for explanations and solutions. This type of intelligence is associated with what we call creativity, or even wisdom.

Claxton is right. Thoughtful reflection on the five dimensions of leadership described in this chapter makes evident the complexity of bringing new life and new insights into the Christian school movement. These dimensions must be understood by all leaders and applied at all levels—within professional organizations, colleges of teacher education, and individual schools. With this approach, and with the blessing of the Lord, great things are possible.

What Do Professional Organizations Say About Leadership?

A number of professional education associations have outlined the skills, knowledge, and understandings needed by education leaders. Public schools in many states have adopted the leadership standards established by the Interstate School Leaders Licensure Consortium, which operates under the auspices of the Council of Chief State School Officers. These standards, which incorporate the best available research on school leadership, are listed below. As you read them, consider their application to Christian schools and the ways Scripture supports them.

Standard 1: A school administrator is an educational leader who promotes the success of all students by facilitating the development, articulation, implementation, and stewardship of a vision of learning that is shared and supported by the school community.

Standard 2: A school administrator is an educational leader who promotes the success of all students by advocating, nurturing, and sustaining a school culture and instructional program conducive to student learning and staff professional growth.

Standard 3: A school administrator is an educational leader who promotes the success of all students by ensuring management of the organization, operations, and resources for a safe, efficient, and effective learning environment.

Standard 4: A school administrator is an educational leader who promotes the success of all students by collaborating with families and community members, responding to diverse community interests and needs, and mobilizing community resources.

Standard 5: A school administrator is an educational leader who promotes the success of all students by acting with integrity, fairness, and in an ethical manner.

Standard 6: A school administrator is an educational leader who promotes the success of all students by understanding, responding to, and influencing the larger political, social, economic, legal, and cultural context.

On the Consortium website (http://www.ccsso.org), each standard is accompanied by a list of associated knowledge and dispositions necessary to comply with each standard and a list of specific performances demanded by the standard. Reviewing these six standards can help you reflect on the dimensions of leadership and increase your understanding of its role in transforming Christian schools to fulfill the purpose of their creation.

CHAPTER 6

Philosophy, Mission, and Vision for the Christian School

Where there is no vision, the people perish:
but he that keepeth the law, happy is he.

Solomon, Proverbs 29:18

EVERY CHRISTIAN EDUCATOR CAN PROBABLY quote the words of King Solomon cited above. But quoting the Scripture is one thing; understanding and appropriately applying Solomon's words to the education of children is another. Let's first look at context. Proverbs 29:18 is related to the verse that precedes it: "Correct thy son, and he shall give thee rest; yea, he shall give delight unto thy soul." This is followed by Solomon's statement about the importance of vision. Taken together, these verses teach that parents' inability to see the connection between today's discipline and tomorrow's outcomes sow the seeds of an unhappy future—whereas parents with the vision to see where things are headed will take the time to properly instill discipline in their children and will reap a good reward for the effort. This truth applies to educators as well, given their role in helping parents fulfill their parental obligation to teach and instruct their children in the ways of righteousness.

Now, let's examine Solomon's words from a scholarly perspective. The word translated in English as "vision" is *hazon*—a divinely given revelation that conveys a foundational truth. Think of that: foundational truth undergirds the body of wisdom available to help us understand life as revealed in the Word of God. If that wisdom is not present in our lives and in our institutions—if it is lost or discarded—a lifeview based on the truth claims of Scripture will cease to exist, and people will perish as a result. "Perish" is the English translation of the word *yippara,* which is the idea of "letting loose, letting go, or casting away." Thus, Solomon is teaching this: Where there is no body of truth as a basis for developing a biblical view of life, people will cast away the restraints of Scripture. Or, without the guidance of truth, people become unrestrained and undisciplined. Therein is a crucial truth that should be understood by every Christian educator.

In the latter part of the verse, the word *law* probably refers first to Mosaic law, but certainly to all truth coming from God. The person who honors that law will be "happy." Some commentators on this verse suggest that "happy" means "blessable," or worthy of being blessed by God and thus having spiritual prosperity. The verse yields great insight for the individual seeking to define mission and vision for a Christian school.

As mentioned earlier, the context for Proverbs 29:18 is one of discipline. But, it is a broad view of that concept. Here, discipline is not merely a synonym for "punishment" but rather gets at the idea of something to serve as a normative glue holding things together. As discussed here, the "glue" or "discipline" is the lifeview of an individual or the moral purpose of a Christian school ministry. A carefully defined philosophy of Christian schooling, as articulated in mission and vision statements, will serve as a plumb line, guiding people in a common direction toward the true north of righteous living. In combination, mission and vision statements provide a framework for making sense of things being proposed for the ministry. These statements begin to define the culture of a Christian school ministry. They clarify purpose and meaning, which are vital in helping a school become an effective ("teachable") learning community. An understanding of Proverbs 29:18 is crucial to understanding that three foundational "building blocks" are essential to a Christian schooling firmly established in the Word of God: (1) a philosophy of Christian schooling, (2) a mission statement, and (3) a vision statement. Having these building blocks in place, and ensuring that they are understood and shared by all stakeholders at a Christian school, is vital for two reasons:

1. Shared vision keeps the Christian school staff focused on those things that will make a school a vibrant ministry for children. Shared vision unifies and motivates a staff to expend great energy in accomplishing the goals of the school.

2. Shared vision is crucial for maintaining program coherence by saying "no" to proposed innovations that will not contribute to the mission of the school and by eliminating programs that do not fulfill the promise shown at the time of adoption.

Who should be involved in writing foundational documents about Christian school philosophy, mission, and vision?

Dufour and Eaker (1998) refer to foundational documents on philosophy, mission, and vision as the "building blocks" or pillars that form the foundation of a school program. These documents provide direction to the school staff and others as they work together to offer a quality education program for the students enrolled in the school.

The factory model for writing foundational documents for Christian schooling would be to convene a small group of educators at the national level to create a single foundational document that would then be distributed to all schools in the system. However, by now, you probably realize that the authors of this book are not fans of the factory model of education decision making, given its past failures. Instead, like Dufour and Eaker, we strongly favor building a learning community in each Christian school across the United States and engaging each learning community in the writing of these documents.

Bennis (1966) speaks of the importance of a "system of values" and a "climate of beliefs" as the staff begins to create foundational documents that establish a moral purpose for the organization. Presented below are our proposed guidelines on who to involve and what process to follow in creating such documents for a Christian school.

1. The leadership of the school and all of the teaching staff must be involved in writing the foundational documents. Parent representatives must also be invited to participate.
2. There must be full and free communication, regardless of individuals' rank and authority.
3. There must be a reliance on consensus, within the boundaries of the truth of Scripture, rather than the more customary forms of coercion or compromise to make decisions and manage conflict.
4. The idea that influence is based on technical competence and knowledge of truth must prevail, rather than the vagaries of personal whim or prerogatives of position.
5. There must be an atmosphere that permits and encourages the open expression of ideas and understandings of guidelines, based upon Scripture.
6. There must be an understanding that a conflict of ideas is probably inevitable, and participants must be

willing to mediate these conflicts within the principles of Scripture.

Leaders should realize that it will take considerable time to write and agree upon the documents described in the remaining pages of this chapter as well as chapter 7. Therefore, time must be built into the school calendar, and into the school day, to accomplish this purpose. Teachers and others cannot be expected to accomplish this important foundational work on their own time. Leaders need to support, encourage, and facilitate the process.

BUILDING BLOCK #1: **A Philosophy of Christian Schooling**

A very practical definition of the word "philosophy" is this: *the most basic beliefs, concepts, and attitudes of an individual or group.* A literal definition of the word is "love of wisdom." In putting a Christian school's philosophy on paper, there must be congruence with revealed truth as stated in the Word of God. Articulating a philosophy of Christian schooling requires a general understanding of values and reality. In the secular world, it would involve much in the way of speculation. For those involved in a ministry of Christian schooling, the beliefs, concepts, and attitudes should be drawn from the truth of Scripture. The authors believe that a philosophy of Christian schooling should encompass three major concerns: (1) the primacy of God, (2) the priority of the Word of God, and (3) the properties of children as created by God.

The primacy of God. Education cannot be complete without some understanding of God, His person, His purpose, and His design for humankind. Why? Because the nature of God is the foundation of all truth. The eternal, infinite Creator of the universe has revealed Himself to mankind in a variety of ways and can be known in a personal way through Jesus Christ.

Paul's concern for the Colossians was that they might know God, "That their hearts might be comforted, being knit together in love, and unto all riches of the full assurance of understanding, to the acknowledgment of the mystery of God, and of the Father, and of Christ; in whom are hid all the treasures of wisdom and knowledge" (Colossians 2:2-3). Solomon proclaimed, "The fear of the Lord is the beginning of knowledge: but fools despise wisdom and instruction" (Proverbs 1:7). Solomon teaches that fearing (respecting) the Lord is the prerequisite to "higher education" in the Christian sense of the word.

Thus, knowledge of God must be foundational in an educational program meant to edify God's children. It is necessary that the staff of a Christian school reflect on what it means to address the "primacy of God" in the school's education program. In writing a statement of the school's philosophy, they must find "common ground" on the biblical issues raised by questions such as these:

1. Given that God is supreme in all things, what are the implications for Christian schooling and children? Consider the words of Paul in Colossians 1:16-18.
2. What is the place of knowledge in the education of children? Study carefully the word *nourisheth* as found in Ephesians 5:29. What is suggested about "building a knowledge base" in children as preparation for life?
3. What is the place of "knowledge of God" in building a lifeview or worldview that conforms to the truth of Scripture? Should a Christian school have as a goal the building of a lifeview based on the primacy of God and the Bible? What is an acceptable definition of *worldview* or *lifeview*? What is suggested in 2 Corinthians 10:4-5, where Paul talks about the weapons of our warfare and the importance of one's knowledge of God in waging the cosmic battle between the truth of God and the lies of the world's system?
4. Since God is supreme in all things, what does this say about responsibility and accountability for the leadership, the teaching faculty, the children enrolled in a

Christian school, and the parents of those children?

5. Who "owns" the children enrolled in a Christian school? How is the concept of "ownership" clarified in Ezekiel 18:4, 20; Psalm 24:1; and Romans 14:7-8? Given these truths, what are the claims that God has on the children in a Christian school?

6. Does the state have a compelling interest in the lives of children? (*Compelling interest* is a legal entitlement enforceable by law.)

7. What does the "primacy of God" suggest for the place of instruction in Bible and applying biblical principles to all subjects of the curriculum?

The priority of the Word of God. One of the great questions of all time is *Why did Jesus come into the world?* The answer is found in Jesus' reply to Pilate's inquiry the night before the Lord was crucified: "To this end was I born, and for this cause came I into the world, that I should bear witness unto the truth" (John 18:37). Jesus said He came **to bear witness unto the truth.** He came to establish, once and for all time and eternity, truth that can only come from Him. In fact, He is that truth. In the Gospel of John, Jesus uses the expression "truly, truly" no fewer than twenty-five times. He says one is sanctified by that truth (John 17:17) and speaks of another Comforter who should come, **the Spirit of truth** (John 14:16-17). The place given to the Word of God is especially important in view of what is said in 2 Thessalonians 2:10 about those "with all deceivableness of unrighteousness in them that perish; because they received not the love of the truth, that they might be saved."

A vital question is this: How should the leadership and teaching staff of a Christian school deal with the issue of truth? This question is especially important in our time, as the very concept of "truth" seems to be on trial and is rejected in the broader culture. In establishing the philosophical foundation for a Christian school, its staff must address the issues raised by the following questions pertaining to truth:

1. What is the final authority in all issues concerning life and living? Is this a matter of conviction, or is it a matter of preference in building a Christian school program?
2. Is it true that all sin can be traced back to "believing a lie"?
3. How is truth to be treated in each subject included in the school's curriculum? How is the truth of the Word of God to be integrated into the curriculum?
4. Is there an antithesis between the truth claims of God and those of the world?
5. Is the primary purpose of a Christian school one of edification or evangelism?
6. How is the issue of "biblical truth" to be treated in the curriculum of the Christian school? Is it different for the several age levels of the children enrolled? See these Scriptures: John 1:17; 8:32; 14:6, 16-17; 17:17; and 2 Thessalonians 2:12. Compare these passages with Isaiah 59:14 and Colossians 2:8. Then, consider the last words in John 18:37, "Everyone that is of the truth heareth my voice."

The properties of children as created by God: The third aspect to be addressed in a philosophy of Christian schooling is not simple. Articulating one's beliefs about the properties of children as God's creations forces one to ask not only *Who is God?* but also *Who is man?* The answers to these two questions form the very foundation for a biblical worldview.

Clearly, the Bible describes the essence of man as a being created in the image of God, yet fallen into a sinful state and under the condemnation of a righteous and holy God. In John 12:25, man is described as having the freedom to choose what kind of life he will value and pursue: "He that loveth his life shall lose it; and he that hateth his life in this world shall keep it unto life eternal." Note that the word *life* is used three times in that verse. In the first two instances, *life* is the English translation of the Greek word *psuche,* meaning the "soulish" life of an individual. In the last instance, the word *life* is used to translate the Greek word *zoe,* meaning "spiritual" life that can be received only from God through a new birth. Thus, there is a soulish life to be rejected, and there is *zoe* life to be sought from God. An understanding of such verses is vital to understanding the properties of children and how educators can expect to impact children and build within them a biblical worldview of life and of living for the Lord. With this in mind, questions such as the following must be answered by a school staff in writing a philosophy of Christian schooling:

1. Given God's ownership of the children and his claim upon each of them, what is the importance of a knowledge base of truth from the Word of God as suggested by Solomon in Proverbs 29:18? Given that God owns the children, what is the claim that God has upon them? Does God have a plan for each of them? See Jeremiah 29:11.

2. Given that each child is a combination of body, soul, and spirit, what are the implications for a system of classroom management and accountability within a Christian school?

3. Consider the difference in these two statements: (a) All children can learn. (b) All children must learn. What do you do for children who do not learn? Should learning by children be the constant that defines what school is all about? Or should the constant be time and the support system?

4. What should be the focus of the educational program in a Christian school—edification or evangelism?

5. Is building a biblical worldview within children a worthy goal for a Christian school?
6. Study carefully Ephesians 5:29: "For no man ever yet hateth his own flesh; but nourisheth and cherisheth it, even as the Lord the church." What is the meaning of the word *nourisheth* in this verse, and what are the implications for an educational program for children?
7. What choices are available to students and parents in matters of education?

BUILDING BLOCK #2: **Mission Statement**

The essence of profound insight is simplicity. The profound yet simple mission statement of a Christian school ministry enables persons involved in the ministry to see through the complexity of leading and ministering in a Christian school to discern the underlying truths of the ministry. A good mission statement should enable one to see what is essential and to ignore the rest. It must identify the reason for the existence of the Christian school. It must answer these questions: *Why do we exist? What are we here to do together?* Or, put another way, *What is the business of our business?*

Research, particularly that of Jim Collins (2001), shows that a mission statement is not a goal; neither is it a strategy. It is not an intention on the part of the professionals in an organization. Rather, it is an **understanding.** A mission statement for a Christian school is an understanding of what the ministry is all about. Collins found that great organizations "simplify a complex world into a single organizing idea, a basic principle, or concept that unifies and guides everything." Good Christian schools set their goals and strategies based upon a shared understanding of the school's mission, as revealed in its mission statement. Inferior schools set their goals and strategies based on a less sure foundation or sometimes on mere bravado. It may take a school staff several months or even years to discover and agree upon what their ministry is all about. The crucial point is this: the mission statement itself must be brief and simple, yet the understanding that is gained by those who commit to it must give direction and insight into the reason for the ministry's existence.

DuFour and others (2010) support the suggestion that "big ideas" unite a school staff in the pursuit of a moral purpose or mission and lead to the establishment of common goals and a clear direction for the school. The first big idea to be carefully considered by the teaching staff and leadership of a Christian school ministry is this: **The fundamental purpose of the school is to ensure that all students learn rather than to ensure that all students are taught**. There is a great difference between a focus on learning and a focus on teaching. It's time for leaders in the Christian school movement to "step up to the plate" and declare that learning will become the focus of everything that is done in the course of the school day. When learning becomes the constant, time and support services become variables that can be manipulated to accomplish the moral purpose of the Christian school.

DuFour and Eaker (as cited in DuFour, 1998) say there is a great deal of similarity among school mission statements. Here's an example:

> *It is the mission of our school to help each and every child realize his or her potential and become a responsible and productive citizen and lifelong learner who is able to use technology effectively and appreciate the multicultural society in which we live as we prepare for the challenges of the 21st century.*

What does this statement say? It expresses a desire that every child in the school lead a successful and satisfying life while contributing to community and country. It further says all children are capable of learning. But is learning the "constant" in the mission statement? Read it again, and you'll see that the word *help* is the constant. "Help" is probably defined in the minds of those working in the school as the time and support offered by those who make decisions about learning. The statement reveals little about the school's expectation of learning and the practices of those who teach at the school. In practical terms, it provides little in the way of focus or direction. Nor does it suggest what the school will do when a child does not learn.

Think about a quality school. How would you describe it? If quality and effectiveness characterize a school, shouldn't one expect that the students attending it will be able to overcome or counter many of the limitations they bring to a learning moment, such as dysfunctional homes or lack of previous successful learning experiences? DuFour and others (2010) suggest it's time to examine assumptions about the mission of schools and to stop confusing the end with the means: **Learning should be viewed as a constant. Time and support must be viewed as variables.**

Think of your own experiences as a student. If you or someone in your class experienced difficulty in school, the teacher might have responded in a variety of ways, depending on his or her own experiences and beliefs about education. Some teachers alter their approach to instruction or provide individualized (differentiated) learning experiences, monitor the results, and keep trying until the student "gets it." Other teachers quickly fail struggling students, recommend retention at grade level, or provide a referral for special services. What you experienced depended almost solely on which teacher you had. McLaughlin and Talbert (2001, as cited in DuFour, 2010) call this the "instructional lottery."

It's not acceptable to gamble with children's education. But that's what has been done in the past, and the practice continues because schools today generally operate on the same assumptions that characterized schools years ago. Preparation programs often do not challenge educators to think outside the box of their own school experiences. But we can challenge ourselves. In transforming the Christian school movement, it is time for those working in the ministry to say, "All children will learn." After all, did not Jesus say in Mark 10:14 "Suffer the little children to come unto me, and forbid them not?" Does that not include all children? If we hope to bring new answers to the challenges of Christian schooling, we must stop asking old questions (e.g., "How did they do it when I went to school?") and dare to ask new ones. DuFour and Eaker (as cited in DuFour, 1998) suggest that the following questions are useful in building a shared mission statement:

1. If we believe all children can learn, exactly what is it that we will expect them to learn?
2. If we believe all children can learn, how do we respond when they do not learn?

Keep these two questions in mind as you review the mission statements discussed below. These statements are from active ministries located in several states. Try doing your own analysis before reading the analysis provided by the authors of this book.

Mission statement 1: The goal of the church of the Lord Jesus Christ is threefold: evangelizing the lost, edifying the saved, and equipping the believer. ABC Christian School complements all three activities, focusing on the youth of the church, three-year olds through high school seniors. The unique ministry of the school is the delivery of academic instruction in an environment that supports these parental and church objectives, rather than in one which undermines them.

Analysis: This mission statement addresses issues of the church more than the school. When the school is addressed in the latter part of the statement, the emphasis is placed upon what the teaching staff and leadership will do, specifically deliver an instructional program in a supportive environment. While such statements are to be admired, they fail to address the learning of students as the prime reason for the existence of a Christian school.

Mission statement 2: ABC Christian School will provide a college preparatory Christian education that is founded on the absolutes of the Bible,

and at a cost affordable to the maximum number of families.
Analysis: This statement seems to restrict (rather than focus) the curriculum to be offered. No attention is given to student learning, and the statement doesn't say what the school staff will do if students do not learn.

Mission statement 3: ABC Christian School, as a ministry of ABC Church, exists to assist parents in teaching students to glorify Jesus Christ in the pursuit of spiritual, academic, physical, and social excellence.
Analysis: This example offers something very desirable—teaching students to glorify Jesus Christ in the pursuit of several dimensions of excellence—and assisting parents is a worthy goal. The mission statement would be stronger if it included a statement identifying "student learning" as the prime mission and specifying what the school will do if students do not learn.

Mission statement 4: Believing that children are a gift from God to parents, ABC Christian School exists to assist Christian parents from Bible-believing churches as they prepare children to live successful, Christ-centered lives through quality spiritual and academic programs.
Analysis: This statement is similar to the previous one. There are a number of truths within the statement (e.g., children are gifts from God, and parents are stewards), and living a successful, Christ-centered life is something to be desired. Yet, quality spiritual and academic programs are effective only if students learn. Again, the statement would be stronger if attention were given to the learning of students and if the staff expressed a willingness to assume direct responsibility for student learning.

Mission statement 5: ABC Christian School exists to ensure that all enrolled students learn. Learning experiences will be focused upon the acquisition of a worldview drawn from the truth claims of Scripture and applied to the spiritual, academic, social, and physical growth of children.

Analysis: Note that the mission statement offers a specific declaration about learning by students. Student learning becomes the constant. That is why Christian schools exist. It also provides direction for the staff of the Christian school in designing learning experiences for children that focus on the development of a scriptural worldview as the basis for growth across several dimensions.

DuFour (2010) says that the emphasis on "learning by students" in a school's mission statement raises four additional questions:

1. What is it that the staff wants children to learn—by grade level, by course, and by each unit of content?
2. How will the staff know when each student has learned—that is, has acquired the knowledge, skills, and dispositions deemed essential?
3. How will the staff respond when students experience initial difficulties in learning?
4. How will the staff enrich and extend the learning for students who are already proficient?

These are questions that should be considered within the context of a professional learning community. DuFour (2010) offers two more "big ideas" for supporting the operation of a learning community:

1. **Helping all students learn requires a collaborative and collective effort on the part of the school staff.** The literature on education leadership is filled with ideas and instructions about how to embed attitudes of collaboration and cooperation within the culture of a school to produce synergy.
2. **Monitoring the effectiveness of a learning community is essential.** The leadership must develop

a results orientation to everything that the staff does. Evidence of student learning must be gathered as teachers attempt to improve performance. Such evidence can be used to assess current practices and to make decisions about proposed changes.

There must be accountability, and there must be positive results. For these things to happen, a strong mission statement—one that states a viewpoint shared by the principal and staff members—is essential. The quality of education within Christian schools should not depend solely on which teacher a child gets in the "education lottery."

BUILDING BLOCK #3: **Vision Statement**

Nanus (1992), who has done much pioneering work about leadership and vision, says this: "There is no more powerful engine driving an organization toward excellence and long-range success than an attractive, worthwhile, and achievable vision of the future, widely shared." Effective leaders work with a total school staff to put in place a vision statement that presents a clear picture of the desired result. A quality vision statement for a Christian school is one that identifies what's possible and desirable while making people eager to lend their expertise and energies to make it a reality. Senge (1990) says that a shared vision *"is a force within peoples' hearts, a force of impressive power...and if it is compelling enough to acquire the support of more than one person, then it is no longer an abstraction. Few, if any, forces in human affairs are as powerful as shared vision."*

According to Nanus (1992), the simplest definition of a vision statement is this: *"a realistic, credible, attractive future for your organization."* A vision statement for a Christian school articulates a desirable destination and inspires the leadership and teaching staff to journey toward it. It offers a future that, in important ways, is different and potentially better than the present state of the school.

The right vision for a Christian school can be so energizing that it jump-starts the future by mobilizing skills, talents, and resources to make it happen. The Christian school movement is in great need of the focus a shared vision statement would bring. DuFour and Eaker (1998) phrase the issue of a vision statement in this way: *"If we are true to our purpose now, what might we become at some point in the future?"* Senske (2004) suggests that writing a vision statement might be viewed as "creating a cause" that is larger than any single person within an organization or ministry. Why is this step so important? Because God has made us in such a way that we instinctively desire to lead a life of significance. We want to make a difference. Christian schooling should be a significant and difference-making experience for all involved.

Preparing a staff to write a vision statement. A vision statement should never be written by leadership and imposed on the staff of a Christian school. Rather, it should be co-created. When the teaching and administrative staff jointly lead the activity, the result will be a sense of ownership of the ideas embodied in the vision statement. In a church-run school, the leadership of the church must also approve any vision statement adopted by the school. In a board-run school, board members must approve it. Parent representatives may also contribute to a written vision statement.

Chances are good that few if any of those involved in writing the vision statement will have been trained to do so. You may wonder: **Is preparation required for those involved in writing, accepting, and formally adopting a vision statement?** The answer is *yes.*

For a learning community within a Christian school, the starting point for writing a relevant vision statement is *attitude.* There must be an attitude of exploration and openness to new ideas. Then, there must be *action.* The first actions will involve gathering information, clarifying philosophies, and generally compiling the best thinking available. Otherwise, the exercise of writing a vision statement may amount to little more than compiling ignorance. A great deal of information about the school is probably available, and this information should be made available to all those who work on the vision statement. The following information should be reviewed and summarized:

1. Historical information about the school
2. Information about enrollment trends, assessments of the facilities, and any other documents produced by external evaluators
3. Previous vision statements, if any
4. Factors within the school community that might affect the school and its programs for students
5. Previous accreditation reports
6. Test results for the past several years
7. Follow-up studies on graduates
8. Effective schools research and the standards of professional associations

The effective schools research can be a valuable resource for those involved in writing a vision statement for a Christian school. Appendix A includes a listing of resources that report findings in this major research field. Give special attention to the recent work of Lezotte and Snyder (2011), who report on the working and re-working of the correlates identified as indicators of school effectiveness, which has been the focus of much research since 1966. It bears repeating that research findings support the assertion that **all children can learn.** Schools control and shape a sufficient number of factors to enable students to master a core curriculum. In the case of a private Christian school, the curriculum would include the acquisition of a lifeview based upon the truth of Scripture.

Of course, the impact of family circumstances and socioeconomic status on student achievement cannot be discounted or ignored. However, individuals who sense the call of God to minister in the Christian school movement must accept responsibility for their role in facilitating learner achievement. **Learning for all** is a worthy and realistic goal for a Christian school ministry.

Factors correlated with school effectiveness, as outlined in the effective schools research, have evolved over two generations of research. The first generation identified the factors needed for a school to be considered effective; the second expands upon those factors that contribute to learning for all. The correlates are identified by Lezotte and Snyder (2011) as follows:

1. High expectations for success
2. Strong instructional leadership
3. Clear and focused mission
4. Opportunity to learn/time on task
5. Frequent monitoring of student progress
6. Safe and orderly environment
7. Positive home–school relations

In *What Effective Schools Do: Re-envisioning the Correlates,* Lezotte and Snyder (2011) describe each of these correlates in detail and provide research-based resources for examining and implementing each of them in a school setting.

Assessing current conditions at a Christian school. In writing a vision for the future, it's important for those involved to have a clear understanding of the present state of teaching and learning at the school. DuFour and Eaker (1998) offer a rating form based upon conclusions drawn from numerous researchers who have studied schools across the nation. The form is designed to assess selected aspects of schools, and it includes a scale for assessing current conditions within a particular school:

1-3   We are not at all like this.
4-7   We are somewhat like this.
8-10   We are very much like this.

Guided by the model of the DuFour and Eaker assessment form, and drawing on many years of experience in Christian school leadership, the authors of this book have developed a similar assessment form for Christian schools. This form is presented here as a tool that Christian schools can use in preparing to write a vision statement.

1. Christian Schools and Change

_____ Our Christian school is modeled after schools in the public system, where decisions are made top-down, with little input from teachers. There is little understanding of any need to change.

_____ Staff members at our Christian school, including the administrative leadership, tend to function on the assumption that things are well and that the achievement of students is satisfactory. There is little need to change.

_____ Teachers in my Christian school get great satisfaction from what they see in the achievement of students. Students must assume greater responsibility for their own achievement.

_____ Teachers in Christian schools function as a unit, guided by foundational documents, while cooperating and collaborating to improve student achievement levels.

2. Instruction

_____ Teachers are committed to their role of teaching. Teachers believe it is the student's task to learn. Teachers can do little to ensure that students do learn.

_____ Classroom activities are dominated by teacher talk. The role of the student is much more passive than the role of the teacher.

_____ Teachers get together for the purpose of collaborating and cooperating in addressing issues of instruction in the school.

_____ Efforts to improve the quality of instruction generally involve bringing in an outside consultant to talk to teachers.

3. Curriculum

_____ Testing provides vital feedback for the teaching staff. Test results are used to make appropriate adjustments in the curriculum. Curricular goals are based on the results of monitoring student achievement.

_____ Students studying the same subject of the curriculum, but with different teachers, often deal with vastly different content.

_____ There is a uniform plan in place that addresses the specific issue of lifeview or worldview in the curriculum. Teachers are well aware of this plan.

_____   Teachers typically work in isolation. There is little effort to build a meaningful conceptual framework concerning the curriculum of the school.

_____   Student achievement testing and measures are based largely upon the academic portion of the curriculum rather than the development of a Christian worldview.

_____   Leadership does not plan for opportunities for teachers to work collaboratively on issues of the curriculum.

4. Structure of the School

_____   Decisions at the school are made by the administrator. Teachers have little opportunity for input on decisions concerning curriculum, instruction, philosophy, and students.

_____   Teachers have little opportunity to work collectively and cooperatively on matters shaping the Christian school.

_____   There has been little modification in the program of the school for several years.

_____   Foundational documents, including a philosophy of education, a mission statement, a vision for the future, values, and goals are in place and provide a focus for everything that happens at school.

For those involved in writing a vision statement for a Christian school, data compiled from the responses to this assessment can provide a fresh perspective on the school's current functioning. They can then ask *What will the school be like in five years if we continue on the path we're on? What outcomes would we like to change?* The exercise of creating a shared vision statement can have a profound impact on those involved. DuFour and Eaker (1998) and Senge (1990) explain that the following benefits can follow:

1. Shared vision motivates and energizes people. It fosters risk taking and experimentation.
2. Shared vision creates a proactive orientation for the entire staff. The staff is no longer satisfied with the status quo.
3. Shared vision gives direction to the professional people within the organization. The staff knows exactly what needs to be done.
4. Shared vision establishes specific standards of excellence.
5. Shared vision establishes a clear agenda for action. Vision will compel courage to act on conviction.

Additional Resources

For additional information about school effectiveness research, see Appendix A. Combined with the truth of Scripture, this information provides an excellent resource for individuals writing a vision statement. For an example of a vision statement, see Appendix B.

CHAPTER 7

Values and Goals for the Christian School

To know wisdom and instruction, to perceive the words of understanding.

Solomon, Proverbs 1:2

Go ye therefore, and teach all nations, baptizing them in the name of the Father, and of the Son, and of the Holy Ghost: Teaching them to observe all things whatsoever I have commanded you.

Jesus, Matthew 28:19, 20a

SUPPLEMENTING THE FIRST THREE BUILDING blocks for the ministry of Christian schooling—philosophy, mission, and vision—are values and goals. It is important to understand how these terms are defined and how they relate to one another.

Values are beliefs that determine the behaviors, attitudes, mindset, and commitments to be demonstrated by those involved in the ministry. Values reflect the collective heartscape and mindscape of the school community, inform its goals, and shape its practices. Values should reflect the truth of Scripture concerning God's view of children and His view of adults'

133

responsibilities for preparing children for life. *Goals* are statements that establish specific actions, timelines, and priorities. They spell out in concrete terms the values-driven path toward realization of the school's shared philosophy, mission, and vision. Goals give focus to the daily operations of the school and establish milestones that serve as measures of progress. **Structural goals** focus on the building of the systemic structure within which the school carries out its educational ministry. **Programmatic goals** establish priorities for the school's curricular and instructional systems.

Each school should write its own value and goal statements—and review and revise those statements regularly. Why? Because the *process* of articulation is as important as the *product* (written documents). After all, it's only after a value statement or goal is put into words that members of the school community can collectively examine it, discuss it, question the assumptions behind it, modify it, and accept or reject it. Engagement in this process should lead a school's staff to seek scriptural guidance, and it is through this medium that the staff can come *to know wisdom and instruction, to perceive the words of understanding* (Proverbs 1:2), and thus weave this wisdom into the very fabric of the school's culture.

The word "wisdom" (*hokma*) appears more than 100 times in Proverbs, generally as an attribute of God, though Solomon provides many practical, day-to-day applications. Above all else, the wisdom of God enables individuals to deal properly with the issues of life and issues of eternity and to hold a biblical lifeview. Thus, Scripture places great value on the acquisition of godly rather than worldly wisdom. Teachers and students alike need to be seekers and learners of such wisdom.

The great commission given to the disciples by the resurrected Christ was to teach wisdom (the way to truth and righteousness) to others: "Go ye therefore, and teach all nations, baptizing them in the name of the Father, and of the Son, and of the Holy Ghost: Teaching them to observe all things whatsoever I have commanded you" (Matthew 28:19-20). In giving this commission, Jesus reminds his disciples that "all power" has been given unto Him "in heaven and in earth" (Matthew 28:18). He has overcome the world, and therefore has much to teach those of us still in it. He provides the strength, and He is worthy of a great commitment on the part of the believer. The commission or task, therefore, is one of making disciples, and that involves teaching them and building up within them a reservoir of knowledge and understanding. It implies that both the mind and the heart are involved in developing "learners" and "followers" of the Lord Jesus Christ. Fostering discipleship is the heart of Christian schooling. It's an undertaking that is expected by God—and one that should be highly valued by all stakeholders.

The reason for citing these verses is to make this point: **The Word of God places great value on learning as the means of building that reservoir of knowledge needed to construct a lifeview that agrees with the truth of Scripture. Learning must be one of the values of the Christian school ministry, and excellence, in all senses of the word, must be its aim.**

The question of whether God expects Christians to educate children in a manner based upon biblical truth is not debatable. Nor is it too much to expect that the ministry of Christian schooling be carried out on the basis of clearly defined goals. And it should be done by people who show behaviors, attitudes, and commitments worthy of the Lord's ministry.

BUILDING BLOCK #4: Values for the Ministry of Christian Schooling

The values of a Christian school are grounded in what the staff believes a Christian school should be. Values, as discussed here, are not to be confused with unexamined assumptions. Champy (1995) says that values are "moral navigational devices." As such, they "become the most important structural elements in the enterprise." Why? Because values for a ministry of Christian schooling should derive their shape and substance from the truth of Scripture. There should be a high standard of behavior for those engaged in educating children. Sergiovanni (1992) says sacred authority and one's passion for it should enjoy wide currency in the world of practice for those involved in ministry. Such thinking may have no standing among those with merely academic conceptions of management and leadership. But in the context of Christian schooling, sacred authority enables a school to build a covenant of shared values. This covenant defines the behaviors and mindset of those involved in the ministry.

Sadly, many relationships within schools, businesses, and other organizations are adversarial in nature, with various parties seeking power for themselves. Such behavior has no place in a ministry of the Lord, where all power and glory belong to Him. Lewis (1990) maintains that values based on sacred authority produce three desirable conditions. First, members of the organization receive emotional assurance and the confidence of conviction. Second, a system of values and beliefs will emerge, based on this sacred authority. Third, those within the organization are stimulated to fulfill the mission, moral purpose, and/or covenant of shared values.

Here are examples of a value statement on which every person called to a Christian school ministry should agree: **All children should be loved, respected, and challenged with opportunities to learn.** If this statement doesn't reflect the reality of your Christian school ministry, your staff will experience dissonance as you contemplate the statement. This dissonance will, in turn, create tension or a sense of discomfort. Within a learning community, this discomfort can be openly acknowledged and discussed. Changes can be proposed, values can be stated and embedded in the school's vision and mission statements, and decisions can be made in the light of God's Word. If a school values all children, its staff will take steps to ensure that each child is served. If a school also values learning, its staff will seek wisdom about ways to ensure that each child learns.

Lezotte and Snyder (2011) suggest that the mission or moral

purpose of a school can become meaningful only as the staff defines and clarifies core beliefs and values. Champy (1995), who has been involved in re-engineering or restructuring hundreds of corporations and enterprises, has identified a small number of values that professionals produce and subscribe to when engaged in organizational restructuring. These values fall into two broad categories— work values and personal values. *Work values* are those that pertain to a work setting. The five work values Champy identified are appropriate and desirable in the ministry of Christian schooling:

- Performing at the highest level of competence at all times
- Taking initiative and risks
- Adapting to changes within the work culture
- Making decisions
- Working cooperatively as a team

Personal values are human virtues that are appropriate to living and working in the larger context of community or society. In a Christian school setting, it is expected that these values will be informed by biblical insight:

- Being open to addressing real or expected problems
- Trusting colleagues and being trustworthy and ethical in relationships
- Showing respect for others and oneself
- Being willing to give an answer for actions and accepting responsibility for them
- Accepting both judgment and reward for performance

Lezotte and Snyder (2011) suggest that the mission and moral purpose of a school can become meaningful only as the staff defines and clarifies core beliefs and values that are peculiar to a particular Christian school ministry. These two authors offer the following example of the relationship between core beliefs and values:

Core Belief	Value
Education is a shared responsibility.	Achievement requires the commitment and participation of staff, students, family, and the community.
All students can learn.	All students have potential that can be developed. Learning by every student is promoted.
Rates of learning vary.	Time required for mastery has no bearing on the value of the learner.
All students have unique skills and talents.	Individual abilities must be identified and nurtured.

The following belief statement is offered as one appropriate for a Christian school ministry:

> *Developing and nurturing a sense of community among all members of the professional staff is something to be desired. In this case, the concept of community means all members of the school staff working together and sharing a commitment in an atmosphere of respect and trust.*

This general belief statement may give rise to the following value statements:

1.	ABC Christian School values an atmosphere in which nonjudgmental listening and the opportunity to express opinions freely are encouraged.
2.	ABC Christian School values shared problem solving at all levels.
3.	ABC Christian School values student, parental, and community input as issues of Christian schooling are addressed.
4.	ABC Christian School values a sense of togetherness among all those working in the ministry, regardless of task or position.
5.	ABC Christian School provides time in the school calendar for staff to work on issues of education; this may include the involvement of able parents to assist in classrooms, thus enabling professional staff to plan for improvements.

Here is another general belief statement that might be appropriate for a Christian school ministry: *Christian school ministries exist for the learning of children.* The following value statements logically follow this belief:

• Student learning is valued as a constant in ABC Christian School. It should not be modified or negotiated away.
• Time and support services at ABC Christian School are valued as variables in planning for learning among all children enrolled at the school.
• Frequent monitoring of student achievement at ABC Christian School is valued as the basis for decisions about both instruction and curriculum.
• Everyone at ABC Christian School values each student as a creation of God, thinks God has a plan for each one, and sees the place of education and learning as vital to that plan.

A review of the literature on value statements shows that such documents can take many different forms and styles. The most important things to keep in mind are these: (1) Value statements are the means to an end. In other words, they should inform the decisions and behaviors of the school staff, and they should inform the school's philosophy, mission, vision, and goals. (2) Values drawn from the Word of God should be the foundation of a values statement written and shared by the stakeholders in a Christian school ministry. (3) School principals should prepare themselves to lead the school staff in creatively and collectively writing a values statement that can be accepted by all stakeholders.

BUILDING BLOCK #5: **Goals for the Ministry of Christian Schooling**

Typically, education goals have focused on inputs (what teachers will do or which programs will be implemented) rather than outputs (what students will learn as a result). Transforming Christian schools to a results-oriented culture will require a paradigm shift, with the bottom line being this: *If students do not learn, the school fails.* School leaders and teachers should be involved in writing both structural and programmatic goals that will lead to success for all.

Programmatic goals. Programmatic goals should be stated in terms of student learning and should be specific and measurable. Once these goals are in place, teachers in the school can work as a team to determine how best to ensure that these learning goals are achieved. They will need to decide how to deliver instruction, how to engage and motivate students, how to measure results, and how to adjust their approach if some or all students don't achieve the learning goal.

Programmatic goals focus on what students will be able to do. Schmoker (1996) discusses programmatic goals at two levels of specificity—goals and subgoals—and provides the following examples:

Goal: Students will write well.
Subgoals: (a) Write an effective introduction. (b) Provide supporting details.

Goal: Students will excel in math.
Subgoals: (a) Describe and understand the steps to solve problems; (b) Compute more accurately; (c) Apply mathematical knowledge to practical situations

Goal: Students will excel in science.
Subgoals: (a) Demonstrate mastery of scientific knowledge; (b) Conduct a rigorous experiment; (c) Make a presentation proposing a solution to a scientific problem

Structural goals. Structural goals related to school improvement are equally important in creating an organizational framework for accomplishing the mission of the Christian school and increasing the capacity of the school to function effectively. These types of goals should focus on building a learning community, creating synergy, and establishing a culture within the school that is dedicated to learning for all students. A school principal should lead the staff in developing this set of goals. Here are some examples of structural goals:

1. Each staff member will make an unqualified commitment to the principles of synergy and community a first step in reculturing the school.
2. Teachers will work with other team members in drafting foundational documents for the school.
3. Time will be made available on the school calendar for teachers to collaborate on curriculum and instruction issues.
4. Achievement by students will be frequently tested, and the results will shape decisions about curriculum and instruction.

Results orientation. How important are results-oriented goals? Maeroff (1993), writing in *Phi Delta Kappan,* suggests that a clear, elevating goal that is focused by a results-driven structure motivates and energizes the professional staff of a school. He further states that it's especially helpful when the goal is shaped by achievement data and when it becomes the focus of a team of teachers. This thinking is supported by Schmoker (1996), who cites evidence that results (in essence, student learning outcomes) are vital to continuous school improvement.

Rosenholtz (1991) points out that the existence of common goals within individual schools is rare. In fact, the lack of specific, results-oriented goals as a driver of decisions and actions makes schools unique among organizations and businesses. Often there is very little agreement within schools about priorities, even though research shows that the presence of goals accounts for progress and effectiveness in improving student achievement. Rosenholtz's research supports the finding that a reciprocal relationship exists between commonly held goals and collegiality within a staff. Without clear and precise goals, a school's staff is hindered in communicating meaningfully and precisely about how to improve learning among students. In this situation, schools become collections of independent teachers, each working in isolation rather than as a cohesive, high-functioning unit.

DuFour and Eaker (1998) report that the "staffs of schools, left to their own devices, have typically been unable to articulate clear, limited, well-defined goals." Schmoker (1996) describes the gap between the need to improve schools and the absence of clear, concrete, academic goals as "the most striking, contradictory, self-defeating characteristic of schooling and our efforts to improve it." Goodlad and colleagues (1970) cite "clearly discernible...clear-cut specified goals for schooling at all levels of responsibility" as an important component of school reform. The absence of such goals, they say, is the most credible explanation for why the profession is still "inching along" in efforts to improve schooling.

Schmoker (1996) reports that a key characteristic of a thriving and healthy learning community is teamwork, and goals are necessary for teams to be effective and cohesive. This is clearly evident from research: Specific goals, rather than team members' personalities or predispositions, promote effective teamwork. According to Little (1990, cited in Schmoker), "The most effective forms of collegiality succeed quite apart from personal friendships or dispositions. Instead, it depends on shared responsibility for a task that individuals acting alone cannot complete." Katzenbach and Smith (1994) add, "Far too many teams casually accept goals that are neither demanding, precise, realistic, nor actually held in common.... Teamwork alone never makes a team." Goals, it seems, are the drivers and markers of progress.

DuFour and Eaker (1998) give special attention to the role of goals in creating clear, discernible victories—not just "hoping for the best." Common goals are vital to any school improvement effort.

Often the issue of school improvement is addressed as "increasing school capacity." In the context of school improvement, capacity has nothing to do with the size of the school building; it has everything to do with the ability of the education professionals to identify the learning needs of individual students, to write specific and measureable goals to address those needs, and to pursue those goals in realistic ways.

Kotter (1996) suggests that some of the goals designed to increase school capacity should be structured to yield short-term victories for the staff. Such victories should be:

- **Visible:** Sizeable numbers of people should be able to see for themselves the reality of progress and the victory gained.
- **Unambiguous:** People should not be able to argue over the results. There should be clear progress for all stakeholders to observe.
- **Related to the change effort:** People should see the relationship between effort and results. If the goal is structural, the nature of the change and its impact on school functioning should be communicated. If the goal is programmatic, progress in the form of improved student achievement should be made evident.

Every school staff needs to experience victories. Both programmatic and structural goals should be written in such a way to enable a staff to experience the satisfaction of accomplishment. Such victories should be celebrated, and the teams most responsible should be recognized.

CHAPTER 8

Teaching: A New Pedagogy for a Recultured School

*Two are better than one...and a threefold cord
is not quickly broken.*

Solomon, Ecclesiastes 4:9a, 12b

Collegiality: the sharing of authority among colleagues; a cooperative relationship among colleagues.

Merriam-Webster, 2009

WHAT DOES A TEACHER DO? If you think this is a simple question with an obvious answer, you might need to think again! In fact, the issue of "what teachers do" has been addressed through a number of major research efforts over the years, including Jackson (1968), Lortie (1975), and Clandinin (1986). Darling-Hammond (1997) says the major finding might be summarized in this way: "Teaching is characterized by simultaneity, multidimensionality, and unpredictability. It involves competing goals and multiple tasks being negotiated at a breakneck pace with frequent trade-offs and with having to deal with many obstacles. Teaching is a juggling act of balancing a secure environment for learning with the present need of acceptable student achievement." This view of teaching recognizes the importance of what goes on in schools and classrooms. It implies that the principal and faculty in a school control the heart of the several processes of education. Further, it suggests that improvements in the education process, and in the achievement of students, can't happen without the direct involvement of those who work in schools.

The concept of teaching as a dynamic, complex activity is a stark contrast to what Darling-Hammond (1997) says is the typical bureaucratic view of teaching: "straight-forward work dedicated to a limited number of preset and simple goals and objectives, easily organized into a sequence of lessons and other activities in the same fashion for all of the students in the classroom." In this view, there is little, if any, regard for persons, personalities, and individual differences. It discounts the skills and abilities needed to effectively plan and deliver an educational program, and it ignores varying ability levels among teachers. It implies that good teaching can be accomplished by anyone who simply follows a prescription.

Which view is more accurate? Is teaching a complex, creative activity—or is it much simpler than that? The answer is important because it has major implications for policy and for the design of school programs. Consider this:

1. The "complex" view of teaching says it's both a science and an art. The science of teaching requires knowledge of instructional and learning processes and the ability to analyze student outcome data to fine-tune and individualize experiences that result in student learning. The art of teaching refers to flexibility, adaptability, creativity, and interpersonal relationships. In this view of teaching, effectiveness depends on all of these qualities, which can be learned, practiced, and improved. It follows that

such a complex and dynamic activity demands an effective organizational structure at the school level—and appropriate support from regional, state, and national organizations concerned with improving education.

2. The "bureaucratic" view of teaching says it's a matter of local schools explicitly following directives issued by people who don't actually work in the school but hold positions of regional, state, or local authority. This view reflects the "factory model" that has characterized the education system in the United States from its inception—the model adopted by the Christian school movement. The bureaucratic view of teaching says that improving educational processes and products is a simple matter of issuing new directives for practitioners to follow.

Which view is more accurate? Decades of research and practice tell us this: **Bureaucratic policies that do not account for the realities of what a teacher actually does in the classroom will in no way promote the modifications in the system that must be considered.** Wise and Darling-Hammond (1984) have produced numerous case studies showing that policies originating in an educational bureaucracy and directed toward classroom teachers sometimes support but more often impede real progress. This makes sense. After all, it's only when decisions about pedagogy are made at the school and classroom levels that they can take into account the strengths of those who are doing the teaching and learning within the school. Significant improvements in Christian schooling must be created and carried out by the administrators and teachers working within a particular school and serving a particular group of students. *There is no other way.*

A new concept of teaching must prevail—one that dispenses with bureaucracy and calls on the collective gifts of leaders and teachers within Christian schools. These gifts already exist in abundance, but they need to be nurtured and supported. How? The case studies conducted by Wise and Darling-Hammond (1984) found that three things really matter to teachers:

1. Having the flexibility to teach adaptively
2. Knowing students well, establishing strong relationships with them, and thereby understanding what motivates them to learn and achieve
3. Focusing on learning rather than on implementation procedures

The impersonal nature of the factory model of schooling works against these three conditions. However, the collaborative, student-focused nature of a professional learning community is fertile ground for teaching practices that focus on student learning.

The research cited above is but one example of a great reservoir of knowledge about teaching and learning resulting from studies conducted in public schools. Although conceived and conducted in secular settings, this research addresses issues that are not foreign to Christian schools. In fact, many research findings support biblical truths. For example, several studies have found that caring, appropriate relationships between teachers and students are important to student learning. Such findings can be very helpful in defining constructive roles and actions for educators working at the national, state, regional, and school levels to support student success.

In Christian schools, "student success" refers to both academic and spiritual dimensions. Bauder (2011) asserts that Christian schools have not typically produced a better academic product; nor have they produced a better-quality Christian. His assertion raises questions worthy of reflection: *Does the Christian school still have a place? If so, what is the contribution that it should be expected to make?* In considering these matters, consider Bauder's further observations: (1) Christianity is a religion of text, and Christians are people of the Book, the Bible. Christianity derives its entire faith and practice from the written Word of God. No authority is higher than the Scriptures. (2) Christianity affirms the priesthood and soul-liberty of the believer. Among other things, this means individual Christians are responsible to know and understand the Scriptures for themselves. There are many helps, but they may not replace the duty of Christians to learn and obey the Word of God.

Keeping the focus on learning is something that must happen at the school level. No outside force or organization can do it. In Christian schools, this means providing quality academic and spiritual learning experiences by developing a new pedagogy for Christian school classrooms.

A New Pedagogy Demands a Renewed Commitment to Learning

Schools exist for learning. Learning must be the focus for every decision made and every action taken in a school. Certainly, all students within a Christian school ministry should be learning new things about their own natures, about the nature of God and their relationship to Him, and about the amazing world He has created for them. Such learning can take place in the context of science, literature, music, Bible studies, classroom discussions, informal conversations in hallways and lunchrooms, and so forth.

But students aren't the only ones who should be continually learning. Professional Christian educators should be doing the same. In fact, they can set a marvelous example for young people by demonstrating what it means to be a life-long learner. Life-long learning means continuing to be a student, to learn and grow personally and professionally, in both formal and informal settings, alone and with others. It means advancing in wisdom and understanding through reading, study, and practice. It means developing habits of mind that are conducive to learning. It also means seeking wisdom and guidance through faith: "Howbeit when He, the Spirit of truth, is come, He will guide you into all truth: for He shall not speak of Himself; but whatsoever He shall hear, that shall He speak, and He will show you things to come" (John 16:13). Growth in teaching requires growth and understanding of the Word of God, understanding that comes through and by the Holy Spirit. A Christian teacher, as a learner, is above all else a learner of the Scripture. Becoming a good learner is the first step toward becoming a quality teacher. Those who are called to serve as teachers and principals in the ministry of Christian schooling should never stop seeking opportunities to learn.

Note that focusing on learning as the mission of a school does not diminish the importance of teaching. Teachers and administrators who are learners enhance the probability of reaching the instructional goals of the school. Those who don't expand their knowledge of academic content, teaching methodologies, learning theory, human growth and development, the nature of change pertaining to schools as social systems, and the processes of teamwork and collaboration become very limited as Christian educators. As a result, what they are able to contribute to their colleagues and to their students is also limited.

Rushdoony (1981) says that continued "learning is a part of discipline." An undisciplined teacher is a poor learner and generally lacks the qualities required for effective teaching. The marks of an undisciplined educator are identical to the marks of an undisciplined learner:

1. There is generally a backlog of work that never really gets done.
2. It's difficult to get started on a task, even if the task is vital to the ministry.
3. Ministry is viewed as something unpleasant, and there's a constant, nagging sense of guilt as the work is ultimately postponed.

How can Christian educators counter the all-too-human tendency to postpone necessary actions? DuFour and Marzano (2011) suggest that teachers committed to life-long learning should develop a mutual support system to build the collective capacity of the total school staff. In other words, they should band together to create a professional learning community. Their commitment to this community will ensure that learning is woven into the school environment at all levels. Collegial support will ensure that no educator has to face tough challenges alone, without the benefit of coaching and support from other educators. The learning that happens within a professional learning community shares the following characteristics:

1. It is ongoing and sustained rather than episodic.
2. It is job embedded rather than separate from the work or external to the school.
3. It is specifically aligned with school goals rather than the random pursuit of trendy topics.
4. It is focused on improved results rather than projects and activities.
5. It is viewed as a collective and collaborative endeavor rather than an individual activity.

The idea of teachers as life-long learners is consistent with Scripture. For example, as Paul mentored young Timothy, he encouraged Timothy to "study to show thyself approved unto God, a workman that needeth not to be ashamed, rightly dividing the word of truth" (2 Timothy 2:15). The Lord Himself was the Master Teacher, and He spent much time alone, in communion with His Father. Individual study and spiritual practice help teachers fill their lamps with oil, so to speak, so that they can share their light with others.

As Christian schools undergo systemic change, develop a culture of collaboration, and institute professional learning communities in which teachers can share insights and practical know-how, a new pedagogy will evolve. This pedagogy will require teachers and principals to become life-long learners and to apply what they know to improve the school and, ultimately, student achievement.

A New Pedagogy Demands Teamwork

The best efforts to improve the quality of the education product will fail if professional classroom teachers lack the commitment and the skills to function effectively. Shulman (National Commission on Teaching and America's Future, 1996) has this to say about the key role of teachers:

> *Debates over educational policy are moot if the primary agents of instruction are incapable of performing their functions well. No microcomputer will replace them, no television system will clone and distribute them, no scripted lessons will direct and control them, and no voucher system will bypass them.*

DuFour and Eaker (1998) observe that the factory model of schooling regards teachers as functionaries rather than professionals. In the light of Shulman's statement (above), it seems that improved learning in Christian schools can't and won't happen unless we improve teacher performance. In other words, school improvement equals teacher improvement. The "old way" of doing things makes improvement difficult, as teachers work in isolation behind closed doors, seldom conferring with one another about the processes of education or exposing their ideas and practices to scrutiny. When each classroom is a silo, it's difficult for a school principal to see that cohesive, well-coordinated measures are implemented to improve educational experiences for children.

The value of teamwork is not a twenty-first-century discovery, but teamwork among educators is a twenty-first-century necessity. Schmoker (1999) cites a relevant anecdote: When Thomas Edison was asked why he was prolific as an inventor, he replied that it was a result of what he called the "multiplier effect." Edison would place a team of inventors near each other to encourage one another so that each member of the team benefitted from the collective intelligence of the group. Smith (1985) reports that Edison's teams worked better and faster than individuals working in isolation.

Katzenbach and Smith (1994) say that "teams—real teams, not just groups that [those in] management call teams—should be the basic unit of performance for most organizations, regardless of size. In any situation requiring the real-time combination of multiple skills, experiences, and judgments, a team inevitably gets better results than a collection of individuals operating within confined job roles and responsibilities." The key words here are "multiple skills, experiences, and judgments." Individuals working in isolation can never bring that combination to any task. Teams of individuals can.

Walling (1994) says that the work of teachers naturally lends itself to collaboration; that academic disciplines are fundamentally interrelated; and that professional development is an interactive endeavor. When collegiality is promoted among a school's teaching faculty, teachers become leaders in the profession of teaching. Collectively, teachers can contribute tremendous insight and energy to the building of quality schools.

The multiplier effect in education is supported by the findings of Newmann and Wehlage (1995). These researchers found that even competent teachers lacked the organizational capacity to raise student achievement—not because these teachers aren't smart and hard working—but because that task is simply beyond the capacity of individuals working in isolation. Newmann and Wehlage further found that significant improvement in schools requires collaboration in applying "human, technical, and social resources." DuFour and Marzano (2011) reinforce this idea in their book *Leaders of Learning*:

> *If schools can only be as good as the professionals within them, and if one of the most important variables in student learning is*

the quality of instruction students receive each day in their class-
rooms, substantive school improvement will create the conditions
that promote more effective teaching in every classroom. The
best way to improve the effectiveness of individual educators is
not, however, through individualistic strategies that reinforce
isolation.

DuFour and Marzano concluded that having teachers continue to work in isolation is the enemy of improvement. However,
there is great promise in creating school cultures that promote
teamwork and develop a collective capacity to improve the learning of children. Without this teamwork embodied in professional
learning communities, school transformation simply can't happen.
For principals of Christian schools, the first step is to create conditions that promote "learning in community" by the professional
staff. The idea is to lead by sharing power rather than hoarding it.
Power sharing promotes interdependence, distributes responsibility for student learning, and establishes mutual accountability for
student outcomes.

A New Pedagogy Demands a Guaranteed and Viable Curriculum

The sine qua non of a school's success is having programmatic
goals that are expressed within the curriculum and shared by a capable teaching staff. The curriculum should reflect a shared sense of
purpose and direction, and it should define specific and measurable
achievement objectives for student learning.

Members of a school's professional learning community must
have the desire and ability to define exactly what is to be achieved
by students. Recent literature on building a viable curriculum frequently makes reference to the concept of "opportunity to learn," or
OTL. When a school fails to guarantee that specific content will be
addressed at specific grade levels as a part of specific courses, students'
OTL is diminished. On the other hand, a cohesive curriculum that

aligns with specific goals improves OTL. For instance, it can help schools determine which textbooks and other curricular materials will provide students with the greatest opportunity to achieve pre-specified learning goals.

In a professional learning community, educators must be committed to helping all students acquire a well-defined set of essential knowledge and skills—regardless of which teacher(s) are assigned to which students. The teaching staff must be committed to helping all students learn the content that has been identified in the shared goals that are spelled out in the curriculum. This level of commitment demands collaboration and teamwork on the part of the teaching staff. Maeroff (1993) writes that teams are vehicles for increasing a school faculty's efficiency, effectiveness, and motivation. A clear, elevating goal and a results-driven instructional system must prevail. Maeroff (1993) points to interdependence between teamwork and tangible improvement in the achievement of students.

The big message in all of this is that buying textbooks and other curricular material is not the same thing as building a guaranteed and viable curriculum for a Christian school. DuFour and Marzano (2011) maintain that the only way a school can guarantee a viable curriculum, one that ensures that students have an opportunity to acquire vital knowledge and understanding, is to ensure that the teachers delivering the curriculum work collaboratively to do the following:

- Study the intended curriculum
- Agree on priorities within the curriculum
- Clarify how the curriculum translates into student knowledge and skills
- Establish general pacing guidelines for delivering the curriculum
- Commit to one another that they will, in fact, teach the agreed-upon curriculum

What do we mean by a "guaranteed and viable" curriculum? According to DuFour and Marzano (2011), a "guaranteed" curriculum assures that specific content is taught in specific courses and at specific grade levels, regardless of which teacher is teaching each course. A "viable" curriculum assures that sufficient instructional time is available to provide each student with an opportunity to learn what's being taught. A curriculum cannot be guaranteed unless it is viable.

DuFour and Marzano further conclude that the traditional approach to curriculum in the United States has not served teachers or students well because it wrongly equates purchasing textbooks with establishing a curriculum for the school. The result has been curriculum overload—trying to teach too many things but not having enough time for students to develop deep understandings about any of it. A study conducted jointly by the National Governors Association, the Council of Chief State School Officials, and Achieve, Inc. (2008, cited in DuFour and Marzano, 2011) found that countries with high performance scores on international tests limit the topics students are expected to learn and organize the curriculum around standards that are focused, rigorous, and coherent. Contrast this practice with what's happening in the United States (and in our Christian schools), where state standards address a large number of topics at each grade level. The study concluded, "U. S. schools therefore end up using curricula that are a mile wide and an inch deep."

Schmidt, Houang, and Cogan (2002; cited in DuFour and Marzano, 2011) agree. Here's how they summarize their findings about the curricula in U.S. schools:

> There are more state standards at each grade level than any other nation…and U. S. teachers cover more topics than teachers in any other country…. Our teachers work in a context that demands they teach a lot of things, but nothing in depth….The goal is to teach 35 things briefly, not ten things well.

Imagine being in a class where you have one semester to read and understand the Bible, and you'll get a pretty good idea of why a "mile wide, inch-deep" curriculum is not the best approach!

So, what's a professional learning community to do? First, guided by the foundational documents discussed in the previous two chapters, its members must establish a guaranteed and viable curriculum. Then, they must work collaboratively in teams to extract from available textbooks only those materials that align with essential learning outcomes for their students, then supplement those materials appropriately. Establishing this level of clarity in the curriculum of a Christian school is a vital step in improving individual Christian schools and in sustaining the Christian school movement.

Here we pause to consider a defining element of Christian schooling—Bible instruction. One might suppose that most Christian schools already have a guaranteed and viable Bible curriculum in place. However, after visiting many schools and serving on numerous accreditation teams, the authors of this book have concluded that the Bible curriculum in the typical Christian school is the area in the greatest need of careful study by the full professional staff. Together, staff members need to identify essential learning outcomes, sequence those outcomes by grade level, and specify the objectives to be achieved by students. The pastoral staff of the church (or the pastoral advisors for a board-run school) should be directly involved as well. The driving purpose should be to help students acquire a lifeview or worldview based on biblical truth. This must top the list of goals and objectives for a Christian school.

In *Leaders of Learning,* DuFour and Marzano (2011) discuss the nature of objectives, the appropriate breadth of objectives as they define information and/or skills, the types of knowledge or mental process addressed by the objective, the appropriate number of objectives to include in a school curriculum, and proficiency scales that should be applied. Their book, published by Solution Tree (www.solution-tree.com), is highly recommended for professional learning communities embarking on the curriculum reform necessary for transforming Christian schools. Several authors affiliated with Solution Tree advocate SMART goals for schools:

- **S**trategies aligned with the broader goals of the school
- **M**easurable
- **A**ttainable
- **R**esults oriented, requiring evidence of higher levels of student learning
- **T**ime bound, keeping within the definition of viability

Identifying SMART goals demands that educators become results oriented. That is, they examine student outcomes to determine whether they are achieving learning objectives. This evidence then becomes the basis for decisions about curriculum and instruction to respond to student needs. Unless results are measured and examined, it's not possible to accurately assess the effectiveness of policies, programs, and procedures adopted by a school. And if no assessment is made, course corrections aren't possible.

Obviously, the pursuit of SMART goals is a process that must happen continually. Is it worth the time and effort? *Yes.* In fact, by working within professional learning communities, Christian educators can quickly become adept at carrying out these goals. This work involves identifying the nature of the objectives selected; identifying the proper breadth, or grain, of the objectives; deciding on the appropriate number of objectives; articulating the levels of knowledge to be attained; and designing the appropriate proficiency scales. When educators do these things, they truly become leaders of learning. The role of the school principal is to enable this work by designating time for it within the school schedule and by securing the necessary resources.

The business of Christian schooling is really the business of the Lord. It's time to carefully and prayerfully examine what we are doing. It's time to establish excellence as the standard. Anything less is not a worthy offering.

A New Pedagogy Demands Improved Monitoring of Student Achievement

Teachers all over America are learning the importance of using performance data to monitor student success. Researchers have found that the impact of monitoring student learning is "nearly linear." In layman's terms, that means more monitoring leads to more achievement by students (Reeves, 2011, cited in DuFour & Marzano, 2011). Reeves further states that effective monitoring of student learning focuses not just on test scores but also on how various teaching practices affect test scores. When testing is viewed as formative—that is, when teachers use the results as inputs to improve curriculum and instruction instead of merely to assign grades—it can have a positive impact on student achievement.

Teaching within a professional learning community means that teachers must become skilled in formative assessment. This type of assessment is done frequently and may take many forms—written or verbal, formal or informal. The resulting data enable schools to make instructional and management decisions on a basis other than assumptions about why learning is or is not happening as anticipated. Frequent monitoring of student performance data is a responsible, proactive approach to improving teaching and learning. It enables teachers to make adjustments now rather than later, when students may need costly remediation—or may have lost faith in their own ability to learn.

Schmoker (1999) identifies the selective and judicious use of student performance data as the third of three vital aspects of a school improvement plan, with the first two being teamwork and goals. Katzenback and Smith (1994) say that teacher collaboration, combined with a focus upon shared goals, does much to enhance the performance of students. What makes teamwork such an important ingredient in school improvement? For one thing, it helps individual teachers become less hesitant, uneasy, and unsure about trying a new or different way to improve learning. Teamwork is also a mechanism for sharing ideas, getting professional feedback, and fine-tuning teaching strategies. Within the body of Christ, teamwork, not isolation, is the model described in the Word of God.

Schmoker (1999) says that educators *do, do, and do*—but seldom study to determine the impact of what is being done. Teachers in a professional learning community need time to reflect on what they are doing. They must become adept at frequently monitoring student performance and analyzing the resulting data to make whatever adjustments are necessary to improve student performance. This conceptual shift is essential to transforming the Christian school movement in the United States.

CHAPTER 9

Professional Development

Study to show thyself approved unto God, a workman that needeth not to be ashamed, rightly dividing the word of truth.
Apostle Paul, 2 Timothy 2:15

Add to your faith virtue; and to virtue, knowledge.
Apostle Peter, 2 Peter 1:5b, c

ACTION IS ROOTED IN THOUGHT. If we hope to transform Christian schools so that they, in turn, can transform students' lives, then everyone involved in the movement must thoughtfully consider what actions will make the greatest difference. The most important shifts in thinking, however, must happen in schools and classrooms rather than in boardrooms. Fullan (2001) goes so far as to say that transformation "depends on what teachers do and think—it's as simple and as complex as that."

Policy mandates and one-shot workshops are generally not the most effective vehicles for helping teachers adopt new ideas about teaching and put them into action in the classroom. What's needed is high-quality professional development that is meaningful, job embedded, and informed by biblical principles and by the best available research on teaching and learning. The professional development experiences in which Christian educators engage must be powerful enough to spark major changes in the cultural and social structure of the school.

Further, teachers' professional growth must also be supported by administrative decisions and structures—and this is where many schools fall short. Fullan (2001) says changes in schools and classrooms become effective when (1) quality people are recruited to teaching and (2) the school is organized to energize teachers and reward accomplishments. These two conditions are intimately related. First, it's important to attract to Christian schools those teachers whose values, skills, and aptitudes are suited to the ministry. Second, the school must be properly organized to build teachers' skills, thus enabling them to improve their service within the transformed schools. The school as a workplace must become very rewarding in terms of moral purpose, monetary compensation, and participatory decision making. The latter demands an understanding of teaching and learning, the willingness and ability to address diverse student needs, a firm grasp of the curriculum and content one is responsible for teaching, and an understanding of the systemic nature of schools.

Supporting teachers' success and professional growth is something that can and must be done for the sake of the children and youth who attend Christian schools. Who's in charge of doing this? Not students, but adults. Crawford (2011) maintains that the problems in education lie not with *students* but with *adults*. Research on teacher performance suggests that "quality of instruction" is the most important element in the success of children in classrooms across America. This finding is confirmed by much of the effective schools research, which shows that the factors necessary to ensure student mastery of the core curriculum are under the control of the local school. In Christian schools, mastery would include the acquisition of a worldview based on Scripture and the mastery of the core aspects of the academic curriculum.

So, how well are we adults doing in supporting teachers' efforts to accomplish the important mission of Christian schooling? Generally speaking: Not very well. The authors of this book, in their work with Christian schools over the years, have observed that the position of teacher is devalued in the movement, and the conditions of teaching have deteriorated. Teachers enter the profession with great hopes for making a difference in the lives of children, but a third of new teachers leave their positions after three years, and half leave after five years (Crawford, 2011). All too often, administrative and staff positions are filled by individuals who have little if any preparation for serving productively in a Christian school ministry. There is often the attitude that *whatever we do, it's better than the other system.* That attitude must be changed. Why? First, because it wrongly makes public schools—not God's expectations—the measuring stick for Christian schooling. Second, it devalues the worth of classroom teachers and makes administrators think it is acceptable to fill vacant positions with "whoever's available." This is a great disservice to students and their parents. Third, it results in Christian schooling losing its attractiveness to the most ardent advocates for high-quality, biblical education for children. The workplace in this movement must be made more rewarding to attract and retain quality people within the ministry.

A knee-jerk reaction to the assertions made above would be to institute stricter hiring and firing policies. But that's a factory-model solution, and it would not solve the core problem of ineffective teaching because the problem is systemic in nature. That is, it involves not only individuals and institutional policies, but also school structure and culture. Christian school leaders must therefore give attention to developing a support system for both principals and teachers to prepare them more effectively in terms of what is currently understood about teaching, learning, and systemic change. The culture of schools must be changed. New teachers must be retained, and the performance of teachers and administrators must be enhanced. As discussed in previous chapters, professional learning communities can play a central role in energizing schools and supporting positive changes in school culture. As Sparks and Hirsh (1997) have observed, improving school culture is one of the chief aims of professional development:

> *Research and experience have taught us that widespread, sustained implementation of new practices in classrooms, principals' offices, and central offices requires a new form of professional development. This staff development not only must affect the knowledge, attitudes, and practices of individual teachers, administrators, and other school employees, but it also must alter the cultures and structures of the organizations in which these individuals work.*

If professional development for teachers is to bring about the desired results at the classroom level, attention must be given to associated changes at the school level. Otherwise, professional development can amplify existing fragmentation of the curriculum and isolation among teachers. This point is underscored by Fullan (1991), who maintains that the greatest problem faced by school leaders is not resistance to innovation, but the fragmentation, overload, and incoherence that results from innovations that are not studied and examined for unexpected impacts.

The quality of teachers' professional development experiences should also be examined. As Lieberman says, "People learn best through active involvement and through thinking about and becoming articulate about what they have learned." Educators are well aware that students can benefit from having a wide variety of learning experiences and opportunities that engage them in solving real problems and creating solutions (Lieberman, 1995). Likewise, teachers and administrators can benefit from such learning experiences. In practice, however, this seldom happens. We waste teachers' time—and ultimately, students' time—when we fail to act on such research-founded insights into effective professional development for Christian educators. That needs to change.

Darling-Hammond (1995) says that teacher development must focus on deepening teachers' understanding of the processes of teaching and learning and of the students they teach. Professional development experiences should be based on current understandings and should result in a new vision of what, when, and how teachers learn. This new vision requires a shift from policies that control and direct the work of teachers to strategies that develop effective schools and increase teachers' capacity to accept responsibility for student learning. Such capacity-building policies enable professional personnel at the local school to create their own strategies and solutions within the bounds established by Scripture.

Critical Areas of Belief about Education

If the movement has lost momentum over the past forty years, it can be recovered, and high-quality professional development will play an important role. Hopes and aspirations for the ministry must be raised, biblical principles and education research must inform decisions, and holistic thinking must be applied. Christian educators need professional development that helps them examine and reshape beliefs about learning, community, and how meaning is constructed.

Modifying what we believe about learning. Christian school ministries are successful when students and members of the professional staff learn. Christian schools fail when students and professionals do not learn. Therefore, the emphasis across the Christian school movement must be on learning among both children and adults. This may be a new way of thinking about Christian schools and their mission, but there is nothing new about the concept of adults needing to continually acquire wisdom throughout their lives. The Scriptures (especially Proverbs) clearly emphasize the importance of learning, acquiring wisdom, and teaching children. Wisdom and knowledge are to be sought, and learning must become the heart of the moral purpose of the Christian school. Lawrence Lezotte (1997), widely recognized as the preeminent spokesperson for the effective schools research movement, declares, "We believe that all children can learn and come to school motivated to do so." This belief does not imply that all children can learn at the same rate, nor do they enter the system with the same levels of readiness. But, it does imply that the mindset of the professional staff of the Christian school must be altered. The expectations of parents who enroll their children in Christian schools must be high since they are enlisting the school to help them fulfill a sacred trust. The effective schools research was undertaken to disprove the prevailing theory that the home was the major factor in determining student achievement (Lezotte, 2011). This is not to say that the home has no influence. But when learning becomes the focus of the Christian school, the assumption is made that the school controls the factors necessary to ensure student learning of the core curriculum of the school. For students enrolled in Christian schools, learning includes the acquisition of a worldview that is consistent with the truth of the Word of God.

It should be noted again that the effective schools research has succeeded in identifying seven correlates of effective schools: high expectations for success, strong instructional leadership, a clear and focused mission, opportunity to learn/time on task, frequent monitoring of student progress, a safe and orderly environment, and positive home-school relations (see Appendix A). Understanding these correlates should aid the professional staff of a Christian school in making wise decisions about professional development.

When the emphasis is on learning, it follows that the planning process must give early attention to identifying exactly what it is that students are expected to learn. To produce a desirable result, the staff must focus on what students are expected to learn and then develop the instruments to measure what students learn. What happens if such actions aren't taken to direct student learning? Results will still be achieved—after all, results are inevitable—but they may not be the results intended or hoped for!

As educators plan and structure curriculum and instruction, they must begin with the end in mind. In other words, they must start by identifying the desirable ends—what students are expected to know—rather than by listing student activities. No matter how great these student activities may look on paper, they are distractions if they fail to direct students to an explicitly stated result. Teachers need to re-envision themselves as *architects of learning* rather than *activity generators.*

Fitzpatrick (1995) recommends consideration of four principles that should guide the identification of the things students are expected to know. These principles also aid the staff in monitoring the results of instruction, which can then be used to make appropriate modifications in the curricular and instructional systems of the school:

1. There must be clarity of focus.
2. There must be adequate attention given to desired ends.
3. There must be high expectations for all students.
4. There must be expanded opportunities for success in student learning.

Instituting learning for all and monitoring to ensure that such learning is achieved represents a dramatic shift in thinking with regard to the moral purpose of Christian schooling. It also signifies a dramatic shift in what is expected of students. It is a new way of gauging teacher performance, and it provides data for making judgments about how well a school is accomplishing its moral purpose. Equally important, it provides data that can be used in planning for professional staff development and modifying the curricular and instructional systems of the Christian school.

Clarifying understandings about schools as communities. Anyone who studies the recent research into schooling and education in the United States will sooner or later come to know the work of Peter Senge, author of *The Fifth Discipline* (1990). The "fifth discipline" is systems thinking. It's through systems thinking that educators can understand the school as a functioning whole rather than as a collection of parts. This is important because a school is more than people, policies, and procedures; it's also a social system with its own culture and interrelationships, and it's within this system that lasting changes must be made. For Christian schools, the fifth discipline is a way to identify patterns within the school community and to understand how the body of Christ is to function in the ministry.

Community speaks of association and relationship. It speaks of joint effort. It speaks of shared meaning on the part of those unified in a joint effort such as Christian schooling. The fifth discipline (systems thinking) provides a framework for examining the social, cultural, and systemic aspects of an organization and the various types of social and spiritual relationships involved. Wise decisions about professional development are most likely to be made when the context of the entire school system (community) is taken into account.

Because educators have not always seen or thought systemically, reform efforts and staff development experiences are often piecemeal and do not account for the systemic aspects of the educational enterprise. For this reason, reform efforts often fail to focus upon those things that have the potential to bring about transformation. There must be a shift in thinking if Christian schools are to achieve significant, lasting improvements.

So how can members of the Christian school community accomplish this shift in thinking? First, Christian educators must begin to see Christian schools for what they are—communities that embody social and spiritual systems and are characterized by social and spiritual cultures. Transforming a school means transforming its culture, and this must be accomplished across the school community with the participation of its members. The "workshop" for doing this work is the school's professional learning community. Within a professional learning community, individuals commit to personal mastery, examine and modify individual and jointly held mental models, create a shared vision for the ministry, and promote a strong commitment to teamwork as the communal nature of the ministry is activated.

In short, transforming the Christian school movement means transforming Christian school communities, one by one, all across this nation. Although this transformation can be supported externally, it can happen only within each individual school.

Understanding what is meant by constructivism.

Constructivism is a learning theory that says people build knowledge and make meanings based on the ideas they encounter and the experiences they have. In other words, when learners encounter new information, they structure or restructure their understanding of that information in the light of previously acquired understandings. According to constructivists, since people have different backgrounds and experiences, individuals process knowledge and create new ideas or responses in unique ways. For the believer, the Word of God would be one of several factors influencing the believer's unique response to new ideas and concepts.

Clinchy (1995), writing in *Phi Delta Kappan,* says that previous legislation such as Goals 2000: The Educate America Act of 1994 adheres to the transmittal view of learning instead of the constructivist view. The transmittal view assumes that students are receptacles to be filled with knowledge and understanding, which are transmitted to students by teachers. Clinchy refers to this learning model as the "banking model," with the teacher depositing information into student brains. A further assumption of the model is that students are passive during the knowledge transmission process but can prove that learning has occurred by regurgitating it on demand.

The typical professional development experience for teachers is based upon a transmittal view of learning. Information is passed from the brain of the expert presenter to the brain of the professional educator. Or, it is transmitted from a textbook or journal article to the brain of the teacher. If teachers are to put this knowledge to use in the classroom, however, they must, at some point, translate it into practice. The dynamic reality of the classroom demands that teachers construct meaning! Therefore, professional development experiences must model constructivist practices. Examples include conducting action research, collaborating with peers to solve real problems encountered in real schools, and applying or creating a new teaching strategy based on constructivist learning theory.

If we hope to bring learning to life in Christian schools, students and teachers alike must be viewed as active participants in their own learning. Sparks and Hirsh (1997) report that "just as young people create their own [learning] structures based on their interactions, so do adults construct a view of what is real based upon their learning experiences and interactions." A great advantage accrues to the Christian because the truth of Scripture can and should play a role in learning.

Needed: A Major Change in Thinking about Staff Development

In recent years, staff development within the Christian school movement has typically been designed in the board rooms of national, state, and regional organizations. Christian educators who attend national, regional, and state conventions generally choose from a selection of topical workshops or seminars given by experts in various aspects of Christian schooling. The focus is on reaching individual teachers or principals rather than entire school communities, and the workshops generally do not address organizational or systemic issues. Additional professional development experiences are planned by the school principal and convened just before the beginning of the school year. These experiences generally don't address systemic issues or school culture either.

National, state, and regional conventions are not without benefits, as they do provide an opportunity for those working in the ministry of Christian schooling to fellowship with one another and to informally discuss various aspects of the ministry with individuals in similar positions in other schools. A variety of workshops provide opportunities for educators to get focused assistance in areas that impact the teaching-learning process. Those who attend also benefit from motivational speeches and sermons given by leaders in the movement. Such sermons help to keep the movement focused in terms of the truth of Scripture.

However, in and of itself, staff development that requires participants to sit passively while an expert exposes them to new ideas or trains them in new techniques will never transform the movement. Such experiences are generally rated on the basis of some happiness quotient (e.g., "How satisfied were you were this workshop?"), a measure that has nothing to do with assessing the workshop's impact on practice or on the effectiveness of the school.

Current research on school effectiveness shows that sustained implementation of new practices requires a much more interactive and communal form of professional development. Participants must be engaged in examining their own assumptions, knowledge, attitudes, and practices. Further, they must have opportunities to examine the assumptions, knowledge, attitudes, and practices of their peers. This is a necessary step in their journey to transforming the cultures and structures of the schools they work in. Those who design professional development experiences need to take this into account and institute the following changes:

1. Change from a focus on the development of individuals to a focus on individual and organizational development.

The Christian school movement has focused upon individuals with little, if any, attention given to the organizational structure or the culture of the school in which the ministry of Christian schooling is being conducted. This must change. Organizational structures and cultures must be altered. For too long the staff of the Christian school has been looked upon as so many individuals. But, individual improvement does not always translate into school-wide improvement. Hindrances to school effectiveness often are attributable to the organizations' structure and collective mindset of the individuals serving on a school staff. The research of Fullan (2001) and Senge (1990) has shown that unless individual improvement and organizational improvement are combined and addressed simultaneously, the gains of one may be overcome by the deficiencies of the other.

2. *Change from the piecemeal approach of the past to a clear and coherent plan for each local Christian school.*

Staff development at each Christian school must be guided by a clear and coherent plan for continuous improvement. By its very nature, school improvement can only occur at the school building level with a school principal who understands systems theory and the necessity of building a school culture that is dedicated to improving the quality of education provided for the children God has placed within the ministry. School improvement cannot be focused upon the latest fads. Rather, it must logically grow out of an attainable and realistic vision for the school. Such a vision statement must be preceded by a mission statement that focuses on student learning and measureable goals that can be used to make judgments about effectiveness. All aspects of the school work together to support the acquisition of the goals, which should specify the desired outcomes for students.

3. *Change from focus on the individual needs of adults working in the ministry to a focus on student needs and learning outcomes.*

All too often, goals for a school improvement program focus on the perceptions of the adults in terms of what they need as they function in the ministry rather than upon the learning needs of students. In keeping with the position that "all students can learn," the focus of professional development experiences for adults should be upon learning by the students and others within the system and upon the modifications of the culture that might be needed to bring about improved student learning. It is not enough to gather information on the effectiveness of professional development experiences by asking the participants to respond to a satisfaction scale. Schools exist for learning. And that would include learning by all stakeholders within the system.

4. *Change from a system of professional development that takes professional personnel away from the school site to a system that is site based and job embedded.*

Sparks and Hirsh (1997) describe much of current professional development as "sit and get" or "go and get" experiences, during which the professional staff is expected to remain passive while an expert verbally conveys information. Such approaches to staff development are generally unrelated to the specific needs of the ministry and the individuals serving within it, not to mention the students it serves. Focus must shift to issues of teaching and learning at a local school, to issues of professional relationships, to issues of working together in teams, and to joint planning. Professional development should be job embedded, relevant to the school's vision and mission statements, responsive to the needs of students, and practiced with the support of a professional learning community.

5. *Change from viewing professional development as something that is "optional" when budgets are tight to something that is vital to school effectiveness and vital to preparing students for life in the twenty-first century.*

All too often, when budgets are tight, professional development experiences are the first things to be cut from the budget. Because a student's experience in the classroom is so vital to school effectiveness, the view of professional development as an "option" or "luxury" must change. Professional development is indispensible to the continuous growth of the professional staff, both individually and collectively, and it is therefore indispensible to the development of students. The central purpose of professional development is, after all, to enable educators and administrators to develop students' innate capacity to learn and grow.

CHAPTER 10

Involving Parents in the Professional Learning Community

And ye fathers, provoke not your children to wrath, but bring them up in the nurture and admonition of the Lord.

Apostle Paul, Ephesians 6:4

And thou shalt teach them [the words of God] diligently unto thy children, and thou shalt talk of them when thou sittest in thy house, and when thou walkest by the way, and when thou liest down, and when thou risest up.

Moses, Deuteronomy 6:7

PARENT AND FAMILY INVOLVEMENT IN education often gets "lip service" but is seldom instituted effectively. This is true for both public and Christian schools. Why? For one thing, "effective parent involvement" is often poorly defined. What is the measure of effectiveness? Is it participation (as in bake sales and school clean-up efforts)? Or is it results (improved student engagement and achievement)? If you recall the previous statements in this book about the need for results-oriented education, it will come as no surprise that the authors advocate results-oriented parent involvement as well! The desired result for Christian schooling is the development of academic achievement as well as a Christian worldview among students. Academics can't be left out of the equation. (After all, the marriage of academic and spiritual learning is what distinguishes the teachings of a Christian school from the teachings of a church). Neither should spiritual education take a back seat to academic learning. (After all, including God's Word in education is the motivating factor for the Christian education movement.) It follows, then, that if parents are to be involved effectively, they must be involved in ways that support both academic and spiritual growth among students. That is the measure of effectiveness for parent involvement.

What Does Scripture Teach about How Christian Schools Can Effectively Involve Parents?

The first place to look for answers about effective parent involvement in schools is the Word of God, which clarifies the relationship between God, parents, and children: Scripture makes it clear that God must be included within the sphere of the family and that parents are directly accountable to Him for properly educating their children. In turn, children are to obey their parents, but they do not "belong" to their parents—they belong to God (Ezekiel 18:4, 20; Psalm 24:1; Romans 14:7-8). There is wisdom in educating children in the truth of God's Word and creating within them the capacity to live for God. Parents are therefore stewards who have been given a sacred trust. Teaching their children is part of their stewardship. Given this truth, parents should not be ignored in matters of education. Christian parents can and should help define the goals for Christian schooling and contribute to the achievement of those goals. This means that parents, in accordance with their individual understandings and capabilities, may be involved in matters of school governance.

The biblical perspective on parent involvement can be summarized as follows:

- God is the ultimate authority within the family, and through revealed truth, He has much to say about the education of children.
- Parents carry the major responsibility for child rearing, and they must account to God for the education they provide for their children.
- Responsibility for the education of children may be delegated, but it may not be transferred to another.
- Both the family and the church have been assigned a teaching function for the next generation of youth.

For people who are followers of the Lord and who accept His Word as truth, there should be no mind or heart disagreement with involving parents, in productive ways, in the education of their own children. In fact, caring about families and involving them is one way Christian schools can fulfill their obligation to children. Children are precious. They are worth the effort. As Psalm 127:3 says, "Lo, children are an heritage of the Lord: and the fruit of the womb is His reward." This verse reminds us that children are a trust from God, and that parents are being entrusted to rear them so that God's trust is satisfied and compensated. A Christian school staff must work within the structure that God has established, and that means caring for children by involving their parents in meaningful ways.

Can parents be involved in ways that will not only benefit the learning of their own children, but also in ways that will help re-establish the attractiveness of the Christian school movement? The authors think this is a real possibility. If a school has established a professional learning community that is working toward common goals, and if parents are involved in establishing and achieving those goals, and if they see that progress is being made, they are likely to get excited about what they are seeing. This excitement can help transform individual schools and re-energize the movement at large. In order for this to happen, the focus of cooperative efforts between schools and parents must be on what matters most:

- Developing within each child a worldview or lifeview that is based upon the truth of Scripture.
- Developing within each child the skills and knowledge that will empower that child to function well in the broader culture and to live to glorify God.

Christian schools are not alone in the quest to effectively involve parents in their children's education. The Center for School, Family, and Community Partnerships has developed six standards for family involvement: (1) welcome all families into the school community, (2) communicate effectively, (3) support student success, (4) speak up for every child, (5) share power, and (6) collaborate with the community. These standards are promoted by the National Parent Teacher Association and are discussed in greater depth on the association's website (www.pta.org). They can be operationalized in Christian schools as follows (notice that we've moved "communication" to the number one spot):

1. **Communication:** Communication between the home and school is regular, two way, and meaningful.
2. **Parenting:** Parenting skills are promoted, supported, and taught by the school staff.
3. **Student learning:** Parents are directly involved at home in helping their children attain the levels of learning identified by the school.
4. **Volunteering:** Parents are welcome within the school, and their support and assistance are sought by the school personnel.
5. **Making decisions:** Parents who can subscribe to the moral purpose of the school are viewed as partners in decisions that affect their children.

6. **Collaborating with the community:** Parents are viewed as a link to the community, and community resources are used to strengthen the school, families, and student learning.

Strong churches are composed of strong families. Therefore, a high level of cooperation between church and family—two God-ordained spheres of the social structure—is desirable. This is especially true when it comes to the education of children, since God has assigned teaching responsibilities to both spheres. Establishing strong Christian schools and involving parents in those schools can be a highly effective way to carry out this assignment and to help young people develop their minds and spirits. Of course, this does not mean that every church should sponsor a Christian day school. It *does* mean that every church should value education and should work with parents in properly educating children.

Two "Thought Traps" Christian Educators Should Avoid

Thought traps are patterns of thinking that prevent a person from seeing the truth or accepting responsibility for his or her own actions. With regard to parent involvement, there are two thought traps Christian educators should avoid:

Thought trap #1: "Not me!" It may be tempting for Christian educators to follow a line of reasoning that goes something like this: *Since parents are responsible to God for the education of their children, and since the conditions in the home obviously influence how children do in school, why should the school be expected to constantly improve and to compensate for what may be lacking at home? Beyond offering classes in a safe Christian environment, what more could reasonably be expected? And the student needs to take some responsibility, too. Who's responsible if students fail to succeed in school? Not me!*

It's true that God holds parents responsible for the education they provide for their children. However, Christian educators must never make the mistake of using this fact as an excuse for offering a substandard education program or a poor quality of instruction. There is only one standard for a ministry that is offered in the name of the Lord: excellence. In fact, the best measure of excellence in a Christian school program is the extent to which the staff is able to help each child overcome various obstacles to learning. If conditions at home are less than ideal, Christian schools are responsible before God for helping children succeed and grow despite those obstacles. The goal of "learning for every child" must be a part of the moral purpose that undergirds the planning of an education program.

Thought trap #2: "Eureka!" Here's another line of thinking that should be avoided: *The reason the students in our school aren't living up to their expectations is that we haven't really involved parents. If we can just get every parent to sign up and volunteer for something, our problems will be solved. We've been searching for the Holy Grail to improve schools, and we've finally found that it's parent involvement. Eureka!*

It's true that involving parents can benefit students and schools. But a strong parent involvement program will never substitute for weak curricular programs or ineffective instruction. Also, parent involvement efforts that focus on parent participation rather than results may not be effective. The reviews of research by Henderson and Berla (1997) identify three qualities of effective parent involvement initiatives:

- **Comprehensive:** The school's parent involvement initiative reaches out to all families, not just those easily contacted, and involves them in significant roles, from tutoring to governance.
- **Well planned:** The initiative includes specific goals, clear communication about what is expected from all participants with regard to those goals, and relevant training for educators as well as parents.
- **Long lasting:** There is a clear commitment to long-term, goal-driven projects, not just one-time activities.

Professional Christian educators should also initiate efforts to involve parents in the education of their own children at home. The professional staff must be prepared to visit homes, to prepare or provide easy-to-read materials about specific ways parents can support learning, and to be sufficiently familiar with the school's overall education program to discuss it at length with parents. Educators must be skillful at soliciting parents' ideas and perspectives, listening to them, expressing appreciation for their efforts, and providing feedback when they ask questions. Educators should be open to the possibility that they might learn something new from parents as well, and they should be willing to use what they learn to help improve instruction and conditions at the school.

What Does Research Say About Effective Parent Involvement?

The effective schools movement is based on two assumptions: (1) All students can learn. (2) The school controls the factors necessary to ensure student mastery of the core curriculum. Research associated with the effective schools movement challenges a long-held assumption that family background is the major determinant of student achievement. As discussed in the previous chapter, this research has identified seven factors associated with school effectiveness, and only one factor ("positive home-school relations") is directly related to parent involvement (Lezotte & Snyder, 2011). However, this finding does not suggest that factors within the home have no influence on student achievement. Ron Edwards, one of the original effective schools researchers, observed that "while schools may be primarily responsible for whether or not students function adequately in school, the family is probably critical in determining whether or not students flourish in school" (Lezotte, 2011).

The authors see no conflict between the assumptions of the effective schools research and other research showing the positive effects of involving parents in their children's education. The implication is that schools can do a great deal to improve learning even when conditions in students' homes are less than ideal—but when parents are actively involved in their children's lives in positive ways, children can do even better! The pivotal role of parents in rearing and educating children is openly declared in Scripture and is confirmed by scholarly research. Christian educators must accept that truth and see parents as partners in the process.

Not all parent involvement in education happens inside the school. In fact, the most important place for parent involvement is within the home. Numerous research studies have explored what happens to student achievement when parents actively support learning at home. For example, when Epstein (1991) studied fourteen elementary school reading teachers in Baltimore who used various techniques to involve parents in learning activities at home, she found a positive and significant effect on student reading achievement. Epstein concluded that teacher leadership by involving parents in planned learning experiences makes a strong positive contribution to reading achievement. This is true even when teacher quality, previous achievement levels, parent education levels, and the quality of student homework are taken into account. This finding strongly suggests that parents can become a major resource in helping children to master and maintain needed skills for achieving in an academic setting—if they are shown specific ways to help their children learn.

Becher (1984) completed a vast review of research documenting the crucial role of parents in the development and education of their children and the ways parents can be trained to improve their children's academic achievement. She found that children with high achievement scores tend to have parents who have high expectations for their children, respond and interact frequently with their children, and see teaching as part of their parental role. Becher also found that parent-education programs are effective in improving how well children use language skills, how they perform on tests, and how well they display appropriate behavior while at school.

The breadth of Becher's review of research on parent involvement enabled her to draw several major conclusions:

1. All parents have strengths and should know that those strengths are valued.
2. All parents can make contributions to their child's education and the school program.
3. All parents have the capacity to learn developmental and educational techniques to help their children.
4. All parents have perspectives on their children that can be important and useful to teachers.
5. Parents should be consulted in all decisions about how to involve parents.
6. All parents really do care about their children.

Becher's findings were confirmed in a comprehensive and definitive study by Henderson and Berla (1997). These researchers reviewed sixty-six studies, including studies that evaluate the effects of programs and other interventions and studies that examine family processes (the ways families behave and interact with their children). They concluded that most parents want to help their children succeed in school, but many don't know how. For instance, parents may not realize that they can help their children succeed simply by talking with them about what they see and experience, reading to them, and encouraging and expecting effort and persistence.

How Can Schools Develop Effective Parent Involvement Programs?

Epstein (2002, 2009) has led a team of researchers in studying how school staffs can develop and sustain excellent partnerships with parents and others within the community. The emphasis of this research is on learning how school, family, and community partnerships can be designed and implemented to improve schools, strengthen families, and help students reach higher levels of achievement. The result of this research is a comprehensive framework that identifies six types of involvement. They might just as easily be described as "six types of caring." The six types of involvement or caring identified by the Epstein model are listed below, and each includes examples of practices that can help "seal the partnership." These examples represent only a few of hundreds that might be adopted by a school staff. Ultimately, each school staff must chart its own plan of action. As you reflect on the six types of caring listed here, consider what might work best in your school and community:

1. **Parenting:** Help all families establish home environments to support children as students.
2. **Communicating:** Design effective forms of school-to-home and home-to-school communications about school programs and student progress.
3. **Volunteering:** Recruit and organize parent help and support.
4. **Learning at home:** Provide information and ideas to families about ways to help students with homework and other curriculum-related activities, decisions, and planning.
5. **Decision making:** Include parents in school decisions and develop parent leaders and representatives.
6. **Collaborating with the community:** Identify and integrate resources and services from the community to strengthen school programs, family practices, and student learning and development.

Although Epstein's framework is based on research done in the public school arena, you can probably think of useful applications within the Christian school movement. The framework constitutes a valuable starting point for creating an effective parent involvement model for Christian schools. Paired with biblical teachings about the vital role of parents in their children's education, the results of creating such a model could be very powerful.

CHAPTER 11

Where Do We Go
from Here?

And be not conformed to this world: but be ye transformed
by the renewing of your mind, that ye might prove what
is that good, and acceptable, and perfect will of God.

Apostle Paul, Romans 12:2

Let this mind be in you...

Apostle Paul, Philippians 2:5a

TRANSFORMATION IS NOT A DIRTY word. It captures the concept
used by the Apostle Paul in Romans 12:2, "Be not conformed to
this world, but be ye transformed by the renewing of your mind...."
Once an individual is saved, regenerated, Paul says that a transformation of the mind, a metamorphosis, is in order. That calls for a
rebuilding of the mind, particularly the conceptual constructs that
are housed within the mind. In this case, it would involve the mental models currently held about Christian schooling for the children
of this nation. We have come to see that this is the "scent of water"
needed to revitalize the Christian school movement.

Know this: we do not desire to assign blame, cast stones, or
lodge charges against anyone. But we do not hesitate to call for

a new discourse among the leaders of the Christian school movement, a discourse which examines both strengths and weaknesses. Serious, honest, and collaborative assessment and study are needed, much along the lines spelled out in this publication. This is the very least that should be done, and it should be done in the interest of the children. There is no greater or more important motive. These children are owned by God (Ezekiel 18:4, 20; Psalm 24:1), meaning that God has first claim upon them. It is a claim that can only be exercised as these children experience regeneration followed by a renewing of the mind, structuring that mind with the truth of Scripture.

The call for a transformation within the conceptual framework undergirding the Christian school movement will demand much on the part of each of us serving in the ministry. Transformation is just that—major change. It is change from the inside out, and that is God's method of change. A bandage or a makeover will not be sufficient. There must be a metamorphosis. Two things are needed for this transformation: first, there must always be a strict adherence to the Word of God. Second, the metamorphosis must also be shaped and molded by what scholarly research reveals about the education of children.

In this publication, we have recommended that schools be viewed as social systems and as cultures, each being unique. The complexity involved in changing a social system or a culture has been discussed at length. We state explicitly that the Christian school movement is also a social system and/or a culture. A metamorphosis within this system or culture must be guided by the same principles recommended for significant change at the school building level.

Changing the Mental Models:

Chapters 4 and 5 of this publication discussed the nature of leadership, first by applying two biblical passages. The first is based upon Matthew 20:25-28, which emphasizes principles of servant leadership. The second is drawn from 1 Timothy 6:11 and 2 Timothy 3:17, each of which shows the importance of a strong moral/spiritual testimony, particularly for those in leadership positions, but for others involved in the ministry as well. Those two principles are foundational. But there is also presented a description of dimensions of leadership, labeled component technologies, one of which was described as Mental Models. Senge (1990) says that mental models are deeply held internal images about how education should be designed and carried out. Unfortunately, the mental images one holds may serve to limit the educational leader or practitioner to familiar ways of thinking and acting. It is quite natural for one to cling to the mental images or models learned over time.

We further state that the metamorphosis needed in the Christian school movement demands a willingness on the part of leaders to examine the mental models currently held about the education of children in a Christian setting. This applies to national and regional organization leaders, to state organization leaders, to those who staff the preparation programs at the colleges, and to both leaders and practitioners at the local school level. Nothing short of that will bring "a scent of water" to the movement.

1. Vision for Christian schooling

> **Lukewarm Concept:** Any Christian schooling is better for children than secular education.

> **Hot Concept:** Quality Christian schooling is essential to the spiritual growth of children.

> The last two decades have witnessed a fading vision, particularly among church and college leaders for the ministry of Christian schooling. Many have become discouraged by the time, the energy, and the human and financial resources that the ministry

demands. Others have lost vision because the results have not been what they expected. In the decades of the 1970s and 1980s, one often heard it said that the movement would soon produce champions for Christ. The movement took on a messianic flavor, and expectations were very high. Needless to say, the movement has failed to produce the results that were once predicted.

But, that does not mean that the original vision was wrong or pie-in-the-sky thinking without a sound biblical foundation. As demonstrated throughout this book, the Word of God has much to say about the education of children. For example, consider the words found in Psalm 127:3, "Lo, children are an heritage of the Lord: and the fruit of the womb is His reward." Be reminded that Rushdoony (1981) offers this insight – "a statist school can only produce a statist mind." That statement is true. Combine that with the words of Proverbs 29:18, "Where there is no vision, the people perish: but he that keepeth the law, happy is he." So, God expects that children be educated to fulfill His trust, presented to Him as His due. Surely a secular system of education cannot be expected to do that. Solomon, writing in Proverbs, says that without a foundation of truth in the minds and hearts of individuals, they will cast away all restraints upon human behavior. But, he that keeps the Word of God will prosper spiritually.

The current mental model in the minds of Christian educators that has led to a loss of vision must be reexamined in view of what God says about the education of children.

2. The local Christian school and hope for the movement

Lukewarm Concept: Christian educators at the local school should implement the recommendations of the board and church leadership.

Hot Concept: Every Christian school faculty will get the training and support needed as they serve as a team in fulfilling the vital mission of the school.

The leaders of the Christian school movement adopted the factory model of leadership in the 1970s, a time when there was much excitement and enthusiasm about the potential of the movement. But the factory model is woefully inadequate for meeting the needs of students at the beginning of the twenty-first century. The model is based upon a concept of standardization and bureaucracy, with educational decisions being made at the upper echelons and funneled down to the local school. There is the expectation that the requirements made in the board room will be adopted by a local school staff and implemented without question. That is simply not true. It further assumes that a school principal and a professional teaching staff of a local school lack the capacity to create a quality education program for children.

The factory model of leadership must be re-examined and, in fact, discarded. The Christian school building must become the locus for planning and carrying out a quality Christian school program. A local Christian school principal and the professional teaching staff of that local school may lack the ability to design a quality program at a point in time. But, the local school is the only place where improvement in education can occur. Therefore, the local school staff must be trained, individually and corporately, to build a quality program. Staff development programs must give attention to increasing the capacity of individual members of the staff of a local Christian school, and at the same time, build an organizational structure to carry out the moral purpose, a shared vision, using a team structure, and promoting collaboration and collectivity by the entire staff to bring about the improvements that are necessary.

3. Learning for each child

Lukewarm Concept: It is the responsibility of teachers to teach. It is the responsibility of students to learn.

Hot Concept: Schools exist for learning by everyone at the school. Learning will be viewed as a constant, and time and support will be viewed as variables.

We remind you that God owns every child (Psalm 24:1; Ezekiel 18:4, 20; Romans 14:7-8). In addition, Jeremiah 29:11 seems to suggest that God has a plan for each one and that He desires the very best for each life. Surely that plan includes an expectation that each child would learn and prepare himself/herself for service to the Lord. Then, the Apostle Paul, writing in Ephesians 5:29, seems to support that idea by encouraging individuals to nourish and cherish themselves in the same manner that God nourishes and cherishes the church.

Can each child learn? The answer is YES. Yet children may learn at different rates and may profit best by a particular learning style. Some children may take more time to learn. But, the point is this: the principle of "learning for all" should guide the effort to transform the Christian school movement. Each child has great potential, and each child can become very useful to God. A commitment to the principle of "learning for all" will serve as a self-fulfilling prophecy for the movement. It will serve as the impulse for building great commitment and dedication.

4. Sustained improvements in Christian schooling

Lukewarm Concept: Improvement in schools and the change it requires is linear in nature and can be sustained by an experienced and committed staff.

Hot Concept: Schools are social and cultural systems. Improvements are systemic in nature and can be sustained only as a new culture is created and shared.

Operating the Christian school movement on the basis of the factory model of leadership assumes that change will follow the issuance of directives from an office or board room that is physically removed from the local school. Research over the past forty years has shown that significant change in education is not easy. It is especially complex when one understands that change is systemic in nature. It involves modifying a social system or a culture of a school or a movement. It entails the creation of a new and different social system or a new culture. It involves an examination of the mental models held by the staff of a Christian school and embraces the possibility of major modifications of them. It involves the development of new relationships among those who meet regularly with students and between teachers and the school principal. It demands willingness to experiment and test as well as willingness to work collaboratively and collectively with other members of the school staff in addressing issues of quality and excellence. And it includes the creation of a curricular system that can be guaranteed and made viable.

But, even that is not all that makes change lasting. The traditional view of the school principal as a manager of the activities of the school must be modified. The school principal must become the cause behind the changes that are mentioned in the previous paragraph. It means the principal becomes a capacity builder, building the capacity of the professional staff to offer a program that is focused upon specific goals, measuring progress toward those goals, and building the relationships among the professional staff members that support this effort. Needless to say, changing a school or a movement is no small task.

5.   Role of Classroom Teachers

Lukewarm Concept: Challenge classroom teachers to improve their instructional and curricular skills.

Hot Concept: Establish a model in each Christian school that taps into the abilities and experience of the classroom teachers, challenging them to work collaboratively and collectively, supporting each other, in carrying out the mission of the school.

Traditionally, teachers have worked as isolates, staying in their own classrooms removed from other members of the teaching staff. But, teachers have great potential. They represent a great untapped resource for planning and carrying out a biblical program of education for children. The factory model now controls much of the thinking about Christian schooling. But it is a model which views teachers as having limited capacity for improving the education offered to children. But, if the local Christian school is to become the locus for the transformation called for in this publication, then professional classroom teachers must be at the very heart of this transformation. The mental model that views teachers as having a limited capacity in bringing about such a transformation is not true and lacks any foundation in research.

Teachers must see themselves as learners, searching for ways to improve their performance in the classroom. They must embrace the concept of working within a team structure to develop a shared purpose for the school. Teams inevitably get better results than a collection of individuals operating within the confined job roles and responsibilities normally reserved for teachers. Teachers must become skilled at writing programmatic goals and doing the necessary monitoring to ensure that goals are being achieved and then using those performance data to make necessary modifications in the curriculum and instructional systems. This role of the teacher is very different from that which is normally seen in the typical school.

One of the most important variables in student learning is the quality of instruction that is available for students. For experienced teachers, professional development programs must become job-embedded. Teacher preparation programs must give attention to new research related to teaching within a professional learning community. Scholarly research now reveals much about the functioning of teachers within the social or cultural structure that characterizes any school. This same research will serve to build great confidence in what the future holds for the Christian school movement.

6. Foundational Documents

Lukewarm Concept: Christian school leaders instinctively know the mission and purpose of the Christian school movement.

Hot Concept: The first step in transforming the Christian school movement into a more vibrant ministry is the writing of the foundational documents for the local Christian school, documents written collaboratively and shared by each member of the staff.

The foundational documents define what a Christian school is all about. Unfortunately, few Christian schools have been defined by a philosophy of Christian schooling, a moral purpose, a vision for the school at some time in the future, a set of values that describe how the staff of the school will behave in carrying out an educational program, and a set of organizational and programmatic goals for the school.

Yet nothing is more important than the foundational documents. The documents serve an important purpose by clarifying and making resolute the answer to important questions about Christian schooling.

Everyone involved in the ministry of a Christian school should also be involved in writing the foundational documents. Everyone must share the philosophy, the moral purpose, the vision statement, the values statement and the goals. These documents, if observed, serve to keep things focused and provide a moral compass for decisions about the daily operation of the ministry.

7. Role of the Local School Principal

Lukewarm Concept: The local school principal is the manager of activities for the school, ensuring efficiency of operation for all school programs.

Hot Concept: The local school principal is a leader of learning, understanding the basic principles of leadership and the nature of instructional and curricular systems, thus leading to positive learning experiences for all children.

There is much research supporting the importance of quality school leadership in creating the conditions for effective and meaningful schooling. Many of these studies focus upon the role of the school principal. Researchers often point to this pivotal position in bringing about the creation of effective professional learning communities. This means that principals are culture makers, whether they recognize it or not.

Persons in this position have a major influence on what goes on in a local school. The school principal should be viewed as the cause behind good things that should characterize every Christian school.

Any serious review of recent research on the role of the local school principal leads to this conclusion: the nature of the leadership provided by the school principal has a significant relationship with the achievement levels of students. One can correctly say this: the more skilled the school principal, the more learning one can expect of the students enrolled in the school that he/she leads. This is because the skills of the school principal will impact the actions of teachers in the classroom, actions which in turn will impact the achievement levels of students.

How are Christian school principals chosen? Persons selected to serve in the role of school principal are too often named through some process of elimination. Sometimes persons are chosen because they are already on the school staff or the church staff, with little attention given to the leadership skills they possess or their knowledge of the processes of education. Needless to say, this does not contribute to a quality Christian schooling program.

There are some critical questions to be asked: What can be done to elevate the status of those serving in local Christian schools, particularly the school principal but also the teaching faculty? What can be done to improve the skill levels of those serving in leadership roles? A new view of the role for the school principal must be embraced and all stakeholders must make the commitments that are necessary to improve the quality of leadership that is available to staff Christian schools.

8. Professional Development for the Local School Staff

Lukewarm Concept: Selecting professional development experiences is a random process with the choice being left to participants.

Hot Concept: Professional development for persons serving in a transformed Christian school movement must be job-embedded and deliverable in a variety of modes and venues to support the development of professional learning communities.

Changing the culture and the organizational structure of an operating local Christian school requires a new form of professional development. It involves instituting new practices in classrooms and in the office of the school principal. This new form of professional development must impact the knowledge, the attitudes, and the practices of each teacher, each administrator, and others who may be sharing in decisions concerning the school. It is a new way of conceptualizing the ministry of Christian schooling. This may be viewed as a daunting task. Nevertheless, that is exactly what must be done if schools are to embrace the mental models that are consistent with biblical truth and the scholarly research that reveals great things about the processes of educating children. These things are needed to bring a "scent of water" to the movement.

Professional development experiences must focus on both individual and organizational development. It cannot be piecemeal. Professional development experiences must be based upon a clear and coherent plan for each local Christian school. It must be job-embedded. Students, student needs, and learning outcomes must be at the center of planning for professional development. Much of current professional development is fragmented, unfocused, and does not address school-wide problems or priorities.

The assumption that schools should embrace the moral purpose of learning for each child enrolled and that professional learning communities should be results driven logically leads to a corollary assumption that professional development should focus upon improving the ability of educators to help each student achieve the defined goals of the school. Staff development experiences can only be judged on whether or not the experiences lead to improved instructional behavior in a way that directly supports the principle of "learning for all."

9. Local Church Leaders and Christian Schooling

    Lukewarm Concept: The task of educating children should be left to Christian educators.

    Hot Concept: Commission a small task force of active pastors, pastors currently involved in the Christian school movement, volunteers for this service, to examine all historical records of the movement for the past forty years and recommend ways to create again the vision and passion once held by pastors for this movement.

Meditate upon this thought: educating children, each of whom is owned by God and for whom God has a life plan, doing this in a manner prescribed by God, and doing it for the purpose of learning by each child, with each child building a reservoir of truth that will enable the child to live in ways that will be blessed by God. The expected end will be a spiritually prosperous life, one that will bring glory to the Lord Jesus Christ. Think of that! When it comes to ministry, can there be a more exhilarating and exciting thought? That is the heart of Christian schooling. Yet, the Christian school movement has lost its appeal, its luster, and its attractiveness. Church leaders are no longer excited about the ministry.

A little more than a quarter century ago, church leaders were enthusiastic, and expectations were high. New Christian schools were being opened in this nation at the rate of three to four each day. Leaders were excited, and the ministry of Christian schooling was promoted from pulpits. Students in these Christian schools were put on display in the schools, in the churches, and in the communities in which the schools were located.

Earlier in this publication, evidence was presented which clearly indicated that Christian schools close because of a loss of vision and a lack of quality leadership. Vision alone will not transform the movement. Yet, vision is important, and it must be restored, particularly among pastors. But it must be accompanied by effective and imaginative leadership at all levels of the organizational structure, at the national organizations, at regional and state organizations, on the college campuses, and in local churches and in local Christian schools. New and imaginative ways must be found to finance Christian schools. New and imaginative ways must be found to elevate the position of Christian school teachers and principals in the eyes of those around them. Preparation programs and professional development programs must and can reflect biblical truth and the findings of research. They must rebuild that sense of excitement about the ministry of Christian schooling. After all, it is a ministry of preparing youth to willingly accept the regeneration that is available through Jesus Christ and then transform the mind with the truth of the Word of God. That is the basis for living a spiritually prosperous life. Can there be any greater service to the Lord? Is not that a pivotal part of the "scent of water" that will lead to a transformation of the movement?

A CALL TO ACTION

Much prayer and meditation have preceded the writing of this last section of this publication. Why? Simply because God has made possible two things that must occur to improve the condition of humankind: the first is a new birth; the second is a transformation of the mind with the truth of the Word of God. Both are critical and necessary. The first involves an act of God quickening the honest seeker and making him or her spiritually alive in the Lord Jesus Christ. The second is a matter of discipleship and education involving the restructuring or the transforming of the mind with the truth of Scripture. The former is a work inside the seeker, a work that only God can do. The latter is the prime responsibility of the parents of children. However, a study of Scripture indicates that the church has been given a teaching responsibility also. Even the synagogue of the Old Testament was a center for teaching and instruction in the truth of the revelation from God.

For the sake of the mission of God into the world and for the sake of the children, the ministry of Christian schooling must continue. It must thrive. It must function to produce young adults who are committed to the service of the Lord Jesus Christ. In the interest of the ministry of Christian schooling, the following call to action is offered:

ACTION # 1:   **Involve Christian educators at all levels in developing a clear vision statement for Christian schooling.**

There must be dialogue and discourse among the several segments of the structure that is presently in place to carry out the ministry of Christian schooling. This dialogue must include input from professional educators working at the building level; input from leaders of national, regional, and state organizations; input from the staff of the institutions preparing individuals for service in the ministry, and input from the churches, including pastors and other leaders. Two ground rules must apply: first, the mental models currently held by participants must be on the table for examination, meaning that no current model should enjoy protected status; and second, the goal of this call for dialogue and discourse must be the development of a vision for Christian schooling that is achievable and realistic, but also widely shared until it connects with the vision statements of local Christian school ministries. Laying out such a vision statement will greatly benefit every segment of the current structure for carrying out this ministry.

The movement has suffered from the lack of a clear vision statement for the Christian school movement. The early response of Christian leaders to the need for Christian schools was characterized as "knee-jerk" in nature rather than a reasoned response to a clear vision for the ministry. As a result, many schools were opened with little, if any, planning or clarification of what the ministry was to accomplish.

ACTION # 2: **Establish "lighthouse schools" that model effective application of biblical principles and research findings within the context of a professional learning community.**
This point has been consistently made: there are two sources of guidance for decisions about Christian schooling. The first is the Word of God. It says much about the education of children, its importance to God Himself, and the responsibilities that are attached to homes and churches in carrying out this ministry. The second is the scholarly research that is currently being done about educating children. That research shows clearly what an effective school is and the correlates that characterize an effective school.

Therefore, a call is extended to seek out local school ministries to serve as lighthouse schools, models for professional learning communities. Such models would require commitments to quality leadership and a staff of teachers willing to work within a team structure to create a guaranteed and viable curriculum. National, regional, and state organizations should seek grants of funds through private foundations or other sources to support this effort. Competitions for these funds would promote the development of programs of excellence all across the United States. The lighthouse schools would serve as models of the truths of Scripture and the findings of research applied in ways to bring glory to God. Excellence is the goal, and lighthouse schools will serve as examples of excellence that can be duplicated many times in local Christian schools across the nation.

ACTION # 3: **Create new models for professional development, models that are job-embedded and supportive of professional learning communities and an updated definition of teaching and learning, models that can be**

delivered in new and imaginative ways.

Updated models of professional development are needed. The thousands of teachers presently serving in the ministry of Christian schooling need new training based on what is known from current research. Initial preparation programs must reflect the findings of that research also. The same would apply to graduate-level preparation programs. This will require that college staffs and practitioners sit together for the purpose of agreeing upon the conceptualizations that will serve as the foundation for updated models of professional development. People improvement equals school improvement.

Specific attention should first be given to improving the quality and quantity of able leadership for the local Christian school. As cited earlier, Christian schools close because of a loss of vision and because of a lack of able leadership. That need must be addressed. The movement must succeed in improving the quality of leadership available, particularly to take advantage of the promise shown by recent research into what works.

Action # 4: **Develop Teams of Trainers for the Movement of Christian Schooling**

Colleges and national and/or state organizations are encouraged to collaborate in creating teams of trainers who can go on-site to local school facilities, to state conventions, or to other sites where groups of professional educators might assemble. The purpose is to train groups and individuals in new methodologies demanded to support a professional learning community. Such training teams might be called "communities of practice." A community of practice could train in an area of common interest, or for a particular position, or play an important role in orienting a staff to several new characteristics of a professional learning community. Other communities of practice could specialize in some aspect of Christian schooling such as writing the foundational documents for a local school, training teachers in how to work as members of a team, training a teaching staff in acquiring performance data and using those data on student performance in making adjustments in the curriculum and/or the instructional system. In this way, the community of practice can embed the training in real situations that will encourage a local staff to become skilled in solving their own problems.

ACTION # 5: **Create written models to guide local school leadership and local school staffs in the processes required for developing professional learning communities.**

Local Christian school staffs need help in first defining and then describing in writing selected aspects of a local Christian school. This call is for the development of written models that should be made available to local Christian schools all across this nation. As an example, local school staffs need help in writing foundational documents, including a philosophy of Christian schooling, a mission statement, a vision statement, goals, and values. Local school staffs need help in creating a positive program for involving parents in a local school ministry. Much research has been done in this area, and that information is available. But, it is another area where a model would greatly benefit a local school ministry.

Such models should not be something to place into the hands of local administrators for adoption. Rather, the model should take the form of instructions for mobilizing a local staff to write these foundational materials. Such documents must become shared documents with shared commitments on the part of a local school staff.

ACTION # 6: **Involve Christian educators at all levels in an effort designed to improve the teaching of Bible and the acquisition of a worldview that conforms to the truth of Scripture.**

Data have been cited that show trends over a period of twenty-two years, data comparing the acquisition of a biblical worldview among graduates of traditional Christian schools, Christian schools that treat specifically the issue of worldview in some way, graduates of homes schools, and graduates of public schools. Some people discount the instrument used to collect these data. But, the instrument has been studied to verify reliability and validity. Those studies are available through Nehemiah Institute located in Lexington, Kentucky. Data on the acquisition of a biblical worldview are available from other ministries. But the authors judge the data from Nehemiah Institute to be the most valid, the most reliable, and the most germane to the concerns of Christian educators.

The trend data shown in Figure 1, found in Chapter 2, should be reason for great concern on the part of Christian educators. Teaching graduates a biblical worldview must be at the heart of the Christian school movement. This call to action would seem to demand immediate attention from college staff, from leaders of national and state organizations, and from pastors. These leaders should create a task force of able people, commissioning them to offer a plan to improve the teaching of a biblical worldview and the teaching of Bible in the Christian schools across this nation. This task force should be on a short timeline with the goal of a plan being ready for Christian school staffs to consider and to adopt by the beginning of the next academic year.

ACTION # 7: **Rekindle the vision for Christian schooling once held by leaders in the movement.**

Pastors must regain a vision for the ministry of Christian schooling. At one time, one could say that the movement was pastor-driven. That is no longer true. Pastors cannot and should not be directly involved in the day-to-day operation of a Christian school ministry. But the vision and support of this ministry by pastors is critical to any transformation of the movement. If pastors do not value the ministry and publicly support it, neither will the congregation that he leads.

It is recommended that a pastor, or pastors, with significant experience in the movement, volunteer to serve on a small task force to review the historical record of the Christian school movement over the past forty years. If an adequate historical record is not now available, one that treats the involvement of pastors and other church leaders, then one should be written. At the very least, any gaps in the historical record should be addressed. That initiative should be started immediately. It is believed that renewed attention to the history of the movement will aid in restoring the vision that pastors once held. This recommendation is offered because of the unique position of a church pastor and the special call from God upon the life of a pastor. Yet, this latter recommendation is offered without hesitation. Pastors must regain the vision they once held for the ministry of Christian schooling.

A second recommendation is this: the task force cited above should also be commissioned to write a documentary, a white paper of sorts, one that explores again the biblical mandate citing the responsibility of an older generation for the education of the younger generation and what occurs in the church and in the culture when that mandate is not accomplished. It might be viewed as a "state of the family documentary," reporting on what is happening to the American family and the state of marriage in the United States. There is much available research to support this concept. Such passages as Deuteronomy 6; Judges 2:10; Psalm 78; and Psalm 127 are cited as Scriptures that should be studied and probed in great depth. This documentary should be widely circulated among the leadership within the Christian school movement.

Action # 8:   Define the logical roles for National, Regional, and State Organizations

At the present time, there are multiple national organizations providing leadership for groups of member Christian schools. That probably will not change and perhaps should not change. There are regional and state organizations performing some aspect of leadership also. The authors have observed overlap of these leadership functions and even some tension resulting from the overlap or the thinking that a certain function can be more efficiently carried out at another level of leadership.

This call for action is one of requesting that a study be completed to determine what leadership functions can more efficiently be completed at the various levels of the organization to carry out the ministry of Christian schooling. The study should be completed in view of the changes in the mental models discussed in this chapter, models that should control the transformation of the Christian school movement. What leadership functions or services can more efficiently be offered at the national organization level? What leadership functions or services can more efficiently be offered through regional or state levels of the organization? What leadership functions and services are to be left for leaders of the local school and the local church? Many leadership functions and services are needed. The matter of efficiency and the wise use of resources cannot be ignored.

References for Effective Schools Research

EFFECTIVE SCHOOLS RESEARCH WAS UNDERTAKEN in response to an Equal Educational Opportunity Study completed in 1966, written by J. S. Coleman (Coleman, 1966). The conclusion of that study was this: family background, not the school, was the major determinant of school achievement. This conclusion prompted a vigorous response in the form of what is called "effective schools research," leading to a research base for the effective schools movement. The result was a body of research that supported the premise that all children can learn and that the school controls the major factors that promote mastery of the core curriculum of the school. Hence, the research led to the **learning for all** emphasis in many schools at the time of this writing. That is the premise adopted by the authors in treating the idea of revitalizing the Christian school movement.

The resources listed below treat at some level the seven correlates of effective schools growing out of this major research movement. The work of Lawrence Lezotte, particularly, has yielded the set of seven correlates from this research effort. The correlates are listed below:

•	High expectations for success
•	Strong instructional leadership
•	Clear and focused mission
•	Opportunity to learn/time on task
•	Frequent monitoring of student progress
•	Safe and orderly environment
•	Positive home-school relations

To be classified as effective and successful, a school must meet two major criteria related to student learning:

The school must show a pattern of overall high achievement.

The school must show a consistent pattern of achievement with no significant gaps across the major subgroups in the student population.

Lezotte, Lawrence W., and Kathleen McKee Snyder. *What Effective Schools Do: Re-envisioning the Correlates.* Bloomington, IN: Solution Tree, 2011.

Lezotte, Lawrence W. *Learning for All.* Okemos, MI: Effective Schools Products, 1997.

Lezotte, L. W., and K. M. McKee. *Assembly Required: A Continuous School Improvement System.* Okemos, MI: Effective Schools Products, 2002.

Lezotte, L. W., and K. M. McKee. *Implementation guide for Assembly Required: A Continuous School Improvement System.* Okemos, MI: Effective Schools Products, 2004.

Lezotte, L. W., and K. M. McKee. *Stepping Up: Leading the Charge to Improve Our Schools.* Okemos, MI: Effective Schools Products, 2006.

Lezotte, L. W., and J. C. Pepperi. *Frequent Monitoring of Student Progress.* Okemos, MI: Effective Schools Products, 2003.

Lezotte, L. W., and J. C. Pepperi. *Instructional Leadership.* Okemos, MI: Effective Schools Products, 2004.

Lezotte, L. W., and J. C. Pepperi. *Positive Home-School Relations.* Okemos, MI: Effective Schools Products, 2001.

Lezotte, L. W., and J. C. Pepperi. *High Expectations.* Okemos, MI: Effective Schools Products, 2008.

Pepperi, J. C., and L. Lezotte. *Clear and Focused Mission & Opportunity to Learn/Time on Task.* Okemos, MI: Effective Schools Products, 2008.

Lezotte, L. W. and J. C. Pepperi. *Safe and Orderly Environment.* Okemos, MI: Effective Schools Products, 1999.

Note: Additional resources on effective schools research may be found at www.solution-tree.com.

Sample Vision Statement

A VISION STATEMENT IS A look into the future. It is a statement identifying what the leadership and staff desire ABC Christian School to become. It should have been collectively written, collectively agreed to, and collectively accepted and shared by each member of the professional staff. The staff must view the statement as a driving force, moving ABC Christian School toward excellence and toward an attractive, worthwhile, and achievable future as a ministry of the Lord and of ABC Church. It is a vital part of the foundational documents defining what Christian education is and what it is to become at ABC Christian School.

It is the task of leadership in a Christian school to promote synergy among the professional staff, providing opportunities and the encouragement to collectively write and develop a sense of ownership for the foundational documents that are necessary to define the ministry.

1. **Leadership:**
    a. Leadership of the school has rejected the "factory model" of leadership that prevails in most schools and has adopted a leadership style that is fitting to the principles of synergy, and to an understanding of the concept of a learning commu-

nity, and to viewing a school as a social system with its own culture.

2. **Students:**
   a. Decisions about student learning are made on the basis of achievement results.
   b. "Learning for all" is accepted by all the stakeholders of the ABC Christian School as the guiding principle in making decisions about students.
   c. Graduates of ABC Christian School have acquired a lifeview that is based upon the truth of Scripture.

3. **Professional Personnel:**
   a. Professional personnel view themselves as "leaders of learning," fully understanding and fully participating in a learning community where shared decision making and shared responsibility, including high expectations for student learning, is accepted and fully embraced.
   b. There is a staff development program in place that has as its major goals the sustaining of the principles of the school as a learning community and expanding the capacity of the schools to serve the students.
   c. Time is available within the school calendar for the professional staff to work on critical aspects of the program of the school.
   d. There is a commitment to excellence on the part of each professional staff member.

4. **Curriculum:**
   a. Decisions about the curriculum are made on the basis of realistic and attainable goals growing out

of the vision statement.

b. There is opportunity for collaboration on the part of the total staff in making decisions about the curriculum.

c. Desired outcomes are clearly specified and agreed to by the total professional staff, and they are communicated to all stakeholder groups having an interest in the ministry of Christian education at ABC Christian School.

5. **Parental Involvement:**

a. There is a well-defined program for gaining insight from parents about the school and its program when that is important and that keeps parents informed about the school.

6. **School/Church Relationships:**

a. The school is viewed as a vital part of the ministry of the church, and the school enjoys the full support and attention of the church leadership.

7. **Community Relations:**

a. The community within which ABC Christian School is located is fully aware of the school and its mission. When appropriate, the community is welcomed to and involved in the activities of the school.

It should be noted that this sample of a vision statement is just that—a sample. Many other major categories could have been chosen. Many other vision statements could have been written for a sample. Each school must write a vision statement that is unique and fitting as a vision of the future for that particular school. A vision statement is critical. It provides direction. It serves as the basis for writing goals for the school, programmatic goals as desirable outcomes for students, and structural goals for building a more effective ministry.

Suggested Readings

DUFOUR, R. AND R. EAKER. *Professional learning communities at work – Best practices for enhancing student achievement.* Reston, Virginia: Association for Supervision and Curriculum Development, 1998.

This work by Dufour and Eaker has probably received more attention and accolades than any other book dealing with educational issues in the last fifteen years. It should be on the desk of every Christian school administrator. It addresses the full gamut of issues related to creating a professional learning community at the school building level, issues ranging from a definition of a professional learning community, the complexity involved in changing a school, to all of the processes for sustaining the changes that are deemed appropriate. It describes an alternative to the "factory model" that has characterized public education in the United States from its inception to the present, a model adopted by the Christian school movement, and a model that has not produced acceptable results. The concept of learning community builds on many biblical principles that should be adopted by Christian school educators. (www.solution-tree.com)

LEZOTTE, L., AND K. SNYDER. *What Effective Schools Do – Re-Envisioning the Correlates.* Bloomington, Indiana: Solution Tree Press, 2011. (www.solution-tree.com)

Lawrence Lezotte and Kathleen Snyder have been the leaders in reporting and describing the results of the effective schools research that was done in response to the report of the Equal Educational Opportunity Study completed in 1966. The major conclusion of this EEO report was this: family background, not the school, was the major determinant of school achievement. This book by Lezotte and Snyder reports the results of the effective school research by describing seven correlates of effective schools, correlates which define factors within the school now known to be related to school effectiveness. Seven such correlates are defined and treated at length.

SCHMOKER, MIKE. RESULTS – THE *Key to Continuous School Improvement*. Alexandria, Virginia: Association for Supervision and Curriculum Development, 1996.

The major premise of this author is simple: *measureable results are the key to continuous school improvement*. Under the right conditions, schools can bring about incremental, even dramatic, results. The author examines each of these conditions in an easily understood and realistic way. He explains the theory behind these conditions that promote significant learning on the part of students. The author would challenge the leadership and staff of any school to replicate the conditions that he describes. Meaningful teamwork, when combined with the development of the appropriate foundational documents for a school, constitutes the foundation for dramatic results.

Educators can begin immediately to provide a better education for all students by focusing unwaveringly on better results and the conditions that promote them.

SENGE, P., A. KLEINER, C. Roberts, R. Ross, and B. Smith. *The Fifth Discipline Fieldbook – Strategies and Tools for Building a Learning Community*. New York: Doubleday, 1994.

This field-book is intensely pragmatic. It includes many

suggestions on how to bring into being collaboration on the part of a total school staff as tough questions about the education of children are asked and studied. There is an openness and mutual respect for all stakeholders within the education community. Each chapter first describes the theory related to the chapter topic and closes with a section entitled "Where do we go from here?" This latter section of each chapter is very practical for the aspiring school leader and staff. Senge, the lead author, is recognized as a pioneer in viewing the school as a social system with its own culture and the strategies needed to make synergy the operating principle in an effort to improve student achievement.

DuFour, Richard, and Robert Marzano. *Leaders of Learning – How District, School, and Classroom Leaders Improve Student Achievement.* Bloomington, Indiana: Solution Tree Press, 2011.

This latest publication by DuFour and Marzano should be on the desk of every Christian school leader. It is based on the assumption that every member of the faculty and administration of a school should be viewed as a "leader of learning." That term, leader of learning," does two things: it assumes that teachers are leaders of learning as much as any other person on the staff of a school, and it places an emphasis not only upon learning by students, but also learning by the professional staff. Student learning must become the focus in the mission statement of every Christian school.

These authors structure the nine (9) chapters around the needed action by school principals and teachers as they create a school program dedicated to achievement of the students enrolled. The book highlights the building of a professional learning community and should serve as a handbook or guide book as that task is undertaken. The book is based upon the very latest research which explores "things that work" and which promotes student achievement.

FULLAN, MICHAEL. *THE NEW MEANING of Educational Change.* (3rd Ed.). New York: Teachers College, Columbia University, 2001.

This author, Michael Fullan, is widely published in matters of educational change. He views each school as a social system, a culture that is unique from all others. Therefore, change in a school is systemic in nature. Any effort toward change at the school level, the only place where significant change can occur, demands that all leaders of learning, and that includes the teaching faculty, must be knowledgeable of what it takes to change the culture of a school. This author, along with Peter Senge, has been a pioneer in efforts to improve the achievement of students in the schools of this nation. One does not have to read far in his publications to encounter this thought: school improvement demands people improvement. That is the heart of significant change in schools.

RUSHDOONY, JOHN R. *THE PHILOSOPHY of the Christian Curriculum.* Vallecito, CA: Ross House Books, 1981.

Though this book by Rushdoony has some age, it remains a classic in addressing the philosophic issues related to the education of children. It will prove especially helpful as a Christian school staff addresses the five (5) foundational documents defining what Christian education really is: a philosophy of Christian education, a mission statement, a vision statement, a values statement, and general goals for the Christian school. Few writers address these issues. The writings of John R. Rushdoony should be available to a Christian school staff.

EPSTEIN, JOYCE. *SCHOOL, FAMILY AND Community Partnerships – Your Handbook for Action.* Thousand Oaks, California: Corwin Press, 2009.

This work by Epstein is the most complete work on school, family, and community partnerships that is available. As such, it is worthy for inclusion in the professional library of any Christian school. Following years of research, Joyce Epstein has developed a six-category framework for examining the nature of positive relationships between and among the professional staff of a school and the parents of the students in attendance and with the community in which the school is located. This framework is comprehensive and includes many practical applications to be considered by a school staff seeking to develop a partnership with parents.

Bibliography

Alsalem, N., and L. Ogle (Eds.). *The Condition of Education*. National Center for Education Statistics. Washington, DC: U.S. Government Printing Office, 1990.

Bardwick, J. "Peacetime management and wartime leadership." In F. Hesselbein, M. Goldsmith, & R. Beckhard (Eds.), *The Leader of the Future* (pp. 131-140). San Francisco: Jossey-Bass, 1996.

Barth, R. *Improving Schools from Within: Teachers, Parents, and Principals Can Make a Difference*. San Francisco: Jossey-Bass, 1990.

Bauder, K. T. "The Christian school." *In the Nick of Time*. Minneapolis, MN: Central Seminary, 2011 June 24. Available at http://centralseminary.edu/resources/nick-of-time/343-the-christian-school

Bennis, W. *Changing Organizations: Essays on the development and evolution of human organizations*. New York: McGraw-Hill Book Company, 1966.

Bennis, W. *On Becoming a Leader*. Reading, MA: Addison-Wesley, 1989.

Billings, R. *A Guide to the Christian School*. Washington, DC: Action Press, 1978.

Blamires, H. *The Christian Mind*. Ann Arbor, Michigan: Servant Books, 1963.

Brown, J., and P. Daguid. *The Social Life of Information*. Boston: Harvard Business School Press, 2000.

Champy, J. *Reengineering Management: The Mandate for New Leadership*. New York: Harper-Collins Publishers, 1995.

Clandinin, J. *Classroom Practice: Teacher Images in Action*. Bristol, PA: Palmer Press, 1986.

Clinchy, B. M. "Goals 2000: The student as object." *Phi Delta Kappan 75*(5), (1995): 383, 389-392.

Collins, J. *Good to Great*. New York: HarperCollins, 2001.

Crawford, A. "Bringing Professional Development into the 21st Century." *Education Week*. (2011, September 9).

Cuban, L. *The Managerial Imperative and the Practice of Leadership in Schools*. Albany: State University of New York Press, 1988.

Darling-Hammond, L., and M. McLaughlin. "Policies that support professional development in an era of reform." *Phi Delta Kappan*. *76*(8), (1995): 597-604.

Darling-Hammond, L. "What Matters Most: A Competent Teacher for Every Child." *Phi Delta Kappan, 78*(3), (1996): 193-200.

Darling-Hammond, L. *The Right to Learn: A Blueprint for Creating Schools That Work*. San Francisco: Jossey-Bass, 1997.

DuFour, R. "Make the Words of Mission Statements Come to Life." *Journal of Staff Development, 52*(7), (1997): 33-36.

DuFour, Richard, Rebecca DuFour, Robert Eaker, and Gayle Karhanek. *Raising the Bar and Closing the Gap*. Bloomington, IN: Solution Tree, 2010.

DuFour, Richard, and Robert Eaker. *Professional Learning Communities at Work: Best Practices for Enhancing Student Achievement*. Reston, VA: Association for Supervision Curriculum and Development, 1998.

DuFour, R., and R. Marzano. *Leaders of Learning – How District, School, and Classroom Leaders Improve Student Achievement*. Bloomington, IN: Solution Tree, 2011.

Eash, S., C. Gunn, and J. Fernandez (Producers), and C. Gunn, and J. Fernandez (Directors). *Indoctrination: Public Schools and the Decline of Christianity in America* [DVD]. United States: Gunn Productions, 2011.

Elmore, R. "Getting to scale with good educational practice." *Harvard Educational Review, 66*(1), (1995): 1-26.

Elmore, R. *Building a New Structure for School Leadership.* Washington, DC: The Albert Shanker Institute, 2000.

Elmore, R., C. Abelmann, and S. Fuhrman. "The new accountability in state education reform: From process to performance." In H. Ladd (ed.), *Holding schools accountable: Performance-based reform in education* (pp. 65-98). Washington, DC: The Brookings Institute, 1996.

Epstein, J. *School, Family, and Community Partnerships: Your Handbook for Action.* Thousand Oaks, CA: Corwin Press, 2009.

Epstein, J., M. Sanders, B. Simon, K. SalinasN. Jansorn, ad F. Van Voorhis. *School, Family, and Community Partnerships.* Thousand Oaks, CA: Corwin Press, 2002.

Fiske, E. *Smart Schools, Smart Kids: Why Do Some Schools Work?* New York: Simon and Schuster, 1992.

Fitzpatrick, J. *Why Christian Schools Close: A Model.* Unpublished doctoral dissertation, Regents University, Virginia, 2002.

Fitzpatrick, K. "An outcomes-based systems perspective on establishing curricular coherence." In J. A. Beane (ed.), *Toward a coherent curriculum.* Alexandria, VA: Association for Supervision and Curriculum Development, 1995.

Fullan, M. *The New Meaning of Educational Change.* New York: Teachers College Press, 1991.

Fullan, M. *Change Forces: Probing the Depths of Educational Reform.* (2nd ed.). London: Falmer Press, 1993.

Fullan, M. *The New Meaning of Educational Change.* (3rd ed.). New York: Teachers College Press, 2001.

"Goals 2000: Educate America Act." Pub. L. No. 103-227 (1994).

Goodlad, J. *The Dynamics of Educational Change: Toward Responsive Schools.* New York: McGraw-Hill Book Company, 1975.

Goodlad, J., M. Klein, and Associates. *Behind the Classroom Door.* Worthington, OH: Charles A. Jones, 1970.

Ham, K., and B. Beemer. *Already Gone.* Forest, AR: Master Books, 2009.

Heifetz, R. *Leadership Without Easy Answers.* Cambridge, MA: Harvard University Press, 1994.

Henderson, A. T., and N. Berla (Eds). *A New Generation of Evidence: The Family Is Critical to Student Achievement.* Washington, DC: Center for Law and Education, 1997.

Jackson, P. *Life in Classrooms.* Austin, TX: Holt, Rinehart and Winston, 1968.

Jacoby, M. "Making the Case for Parochial Schools." *The Boston Globe.* (2004, May 9). Available at http://www.boston.com/news/globe/editorialopinion/oped/articles/2004/05/09making_the_case_for_parochial_schools/

Jennings, J., and D. Rentner, D. "Ten Big Effects of the No Child Left Behind Act on Public Schools." *Phi Delta Kappan, 88*(2), (2006 October): 110-113.

Katzenbach, J. R., and D. K. Smith. *The Wisdom of Teams.* New York: Harper Business, 1994.

Kienel, P. A. *The Christian School: Why It Is Right for Your Child.* Wheaton, IL: Victor Books, 1974.

Kotter, J. *Leading Change.* Boston: Harvard Business School Press, 1996.

Kouzes, J., and B. Posner. *Leadership Challenge* (3rd ed.). San Francisco: Jossey-Bass, 2002.

Kouzes, J., and B. Posner. *Encouraging the Heart: A Leader's Guide to Rewarding and Recognizing Others.* San Francisco: Jossey-Bass, 1998.

Lam, D. *Reinventing School Leadership – Humble Pie.* Cambridge, MA: National Center for Education Leadership, Harvard University, 1990.

Lezotte, L. *Learning for All.* Okemos, Michigan: Effective Schools Products, Ltd, 1997.

Lezotte, L., and K. Snyder *What Effective Schools Do: Re-envisioning the Correlates.* Bloomington, IN: Solution Tree, 2011.

Liebermann, A. "Practices that Support Teacher Development." *Phi Delta Kappan* 76(8), (1995): 91-596.

Lips, D. "A Nation Still at Risk: The Case for Federalism and School Choice." Heritage Foundation *Backgrounder #2125.* (2008, April 21). Available at http://www.heritage.org/research/reports/2008/04/a-nation-still-at-risk-the-case-for-federalism-and-school-choice

Lortie, D. *Schoolteacher: A Sociological Study.* Chicago: University of Chicago Press, 1975.

Maeroff, G. "Building teams to rebuild schools." *Phi Delta Kappan* 74(7), (March 1993): 512-519.

Marris, P. *Loss and Change.* New York: Anchor Press/Doubleday, 1975.

McLaughlin, M., and J. Talbert. *Professional Communities and the Work of High School Teaching.* Chicago: University of Chicago Press, 2001.

McNeil, M. "Duncan: 82 percent of schools could be 'failing' this year." *Education Week.* (2011, March 9).

Miles, M. B. "Unraveling the mystery of institutionalization." *Educational Leadership, 41*(3), (1983): 14-19.

Murphy, J., C. Evertson, and M. Radnofsky. "Restructuring Schools: Fourteen elementary and secondary teachers' perspectives on reform." *The Elementary School Journal, 92*(2), (1991): 135-148.

Nanus, B. *Visionary Leadership: Creating a Compelling Sense of Direction for Your Organization.* San Francisco: Jossey-Bass, 1992.

National Center for Education Statistics. *High school students ten years after "A Nation at Risk."* Washington, DC: U.S. Department of Education, Office of Educational Research and Improvement, (May 1995).

National Center for Education Statistics. *Actual and projected numbers for enrollment in private schools, 1992-2017.* Washington, DC: U. S. Department of Education, Office of Educational Research and Improvement, (2005). Available at http://nces.ed.gov/programs/projections/projections2017/tables/table_01.a

National Center for Education Statistics. *1.5 million homeschooled students in the United States in 2007.* Issue Brief 2009-030. Washington, DC: U.S. Department of Education, Office of Educational Research and Improvement. (2008, December). Available at http://nces.ed.gov/pubs2009/2009030.pdf

National Commission on Excellence in Education. *A nation at risk: The imperative for educational reform.* Washington, DC: U.S. Department of Education. (1983, April).

National Commission on Teaching and America's Future. *What matters most: Teaching for America's future.* New York: Author, 1996.

National Governors Association, Council of Chief State School Officers, & Achieve, Inc. *Benchmarking for success: Ensuring U. S. students receive a world-class education.* Washington, DC: National Governors Association. (2008> Accessed at www.corestandards.org/assets/0812BENCHMARKING.pdf

National PTA. *National standards for parent/family involvement programs.* Chicago, IL: Author, 1997.

Newmann, F., and Associates. *Authentic achievement: Restructuring schools for intellectual quality.* San Francisco: Jossey-Bass, 1996.

Newmann, F., B. King, and P. Youngs. *Professional development that addresses school capacity.* Paper presented at the annual meeting of the American Educational Research Association, New Orleans, LA. (2000, April).

Newmann, F., and G. Wehlage. *Successful school restructuring.* Madison: University of Wisconsin, 1995.

Newmann, F., and G. Wehlage. *Successful restructuring: A report to the public and educators by the center for Restructuring Schools.* Madison: University of Wisconsin, 1998.

Nonaka, I., and H. Takeuchi. *The knowledge-creating company.* New York: Oxford University Press, 1995.

North Central Regional Educational Laboratory. *Summary of Goals 2000: Educate America Act.* Available at http://www.ncrel. org/sdrs/areas/issues/envrnmnt/stw/sw0goals.htm

Paris, K. *A leadership model for planning and implementing change for school-to-work transition (pp. 22-25),* Madison, WI: University of Wisconsin-Madison, Center on Education and Work, 1994.

Pascale, R., M. Millemann and L. Gioja. *Surfing the edge of chaos.* New York: Crown Business Publishing, 2000.

Pottruck, D. "New world, old traditions." *The Chief Executive 161,* (2000 November): 36-40.

Ray, B. *An evaluation of the validity and reliability of The PEERS test.* Lexington, KY: Nehemiah Institute, 1995.

Reeves, D. *Finding your leadership focus: Transforming professional learning into student results, K-12.* Thousand Oaks, CA: Corwin Press, 2011.

Rosenholtz, S. *Teacher's workplace: The social organization of schools.* New York: Teachers College Press, 1991.

Rushdoony, J. *The philosophy of the Christian curriculum.* Vallecito, CA: Ross House Books, 1981.

Salisbury, D., and D. Conner. "How to succeed as manager of an educational change project." *Educational Technology, 34*(6), (1999): 12-19.

Schmoker, M. *Results: The key to continuous school improvement.* Alexandria, VA: Association for Supervision and Curriculum Development, 1996.

Schon, D. *Beyond the stable state.* New York: Norton, 1971.

Selznick, P. *Leadership in Administration.* Berkeley: University of California Press, 1957.

Senge, P. M. *The Fifth Discipline. The Art & Practice of the Learning Organization.* New York: Currency Doubleday, 1990.

Senske, K. *Executive Values: A Christian Approach to Organizational Leadership.* Minneapolis, MN: Augsburg Books, 2003.

Sergiovanni, T. *Moral Leadership: Getting to the Heart of School Improvement.* San Francisco: Jossey-Bass, 1992.

Sergiovanni, T. *The Principalship.* Boston: Allyn and Bacon, 1995.

Sergiovanni. T. *The Lifeworld of Leadership: Creating Culture, Community, and Personal Meaning in Our Schools.* San Francisco: Jossey-Bass, 2000.

Smith, P. *America Enters the World.* New York: McGraw-Hill, 1985.

Smithwick, Dan. *Worldview Peers Study.* Lexington, KY: Nehemiah Institute, 2002.

Sparks, D., and S. Hirsh. *A New Vision for Staff Development.* Oxford, OH: National Staff Development Council and Alexandria, VA: Association for Supervision and Curriculum Development, 1997.

Stackhouse, J. G., Jr. *Humble Apologetics.* New York: Oxford University Press, 2002.

Testimony before House Education Subcommittee on Early Childhood, Elementary and Secondary Education, United States House of Representatives, 112th Cong. (2011) (testimony of Jennifer A. Marshall). Available at http://edworkforce.house.gov/UploadedFiles/03.15.11_marshall.pdf

The No Child Left Behind Act of 2001. Pub. L. No. 103-227 (1994).

Tyack, D. *The One Best System.* Cambridge, MA: Harvard University Press, 1979.

U.S. Department of Education. *A Nation Accountable: Twenty-five Years after A Nation at Risk.* Washington, DC: Author. (2008). Available at http://www.ed.gov/rschstat/research/pubs/accountable/accountable.pdf

Von Krogh, G., K. Ichijo and I. Nonaka. *Enabling Knowledge Creation:*

How to Unlock the Mystery of Tacit Knowledge and Release the Power of Innovation. Oxford: Oxford University Press, 2000.

Walling, D. R. (Ed.). *Teachers as Leaders: Perspectives on the Professional Development of Teachers.* Bloomington, IN: Phi Delta Kappa Educational Foundation, 1994.

Wise, A., L. Darling-Hammond, M. McLaughlin and H. Bernstein. *Case Studies for Teacher Evaluation: A Study of Effective Practices.* Santa Monica, CA: Rand, 1984.

Authors Index

Topic Index

For more information about
EDWARD EARWOOD AND PHIL SUITER
&
A SCENT OF WATER
please visit:

www.christianschoolpublications.com
ascentofwater@christianeducation.org
www.facebook.com/AScentofWater
@AScentofWater

For more information about
AMBASSADOR INTERNATIONAL
please visit:

www.ambassador-international.com
@AmbassadorIntl
www.facebook.com/AmbassadorIntl

41843078R00133

Made in the USA
Lexington, KY
11 June 2019